GW01607915

An ENDOWMENT of LOVE

An ENDOWMENT of LOVE

Embracing Christ's Covenant Way of Living and Loving

MELINDA WHEELWRIGHT BROWN

SALT LAKE CITY, UTAH

Visit us at deseretbook.com

Library of Congress Cataloging-in-Publication Data

Names: Brown, Melinda Wheelwright, 1970– author.
Title: An endowment of love : embracing Christ's covenant way of living and loving / Melinda Wheelwright Brown.
Description: Salt Lake City, Utah : Deseret Book, [2025] | Includes bibliographical references | Summary: "Latter-day Saint author Melinda Wheelwright Brown discusses ways to members to approach temple worship in The Church of Jesus Christ of Latter-day Saints"—Provided by publisher
Identifiers: LCCN 2024054337 (print) | LCCN 202405 (ebook) | ISBN 9781639934188 (hardback) | ISBN 9781649334268 (ebook)
Subjects: The Church of Jesus Christ of Latter-day Saints—Doctrines | Temple endowments (Latter Day Saint doctrine) | Christian Life—Latter Day Saint authors
Classification: LCC BX8643.T4 B765 2025 (print) | LCC BX8643.T4 (ebook) | DDC 264/.09332—dc23/eng/20250109
LC record available at https://lccn.loc.gov/2024054337
LC ebook record available at https://lccn.loc.gov/2024054338

Printed in Canada
PubLitho

10 9 8 7 6 5 4 3 2

To my spectacular Temple+ students,
and to those who've generously made space
for us to learn together.

But this shall be the covenant
that I will make with the house of Israel;
After those days, saith the Lord,
I will put my law in their inward parts,
and write it in their hearts;
and will be their God,
and they shall be my people.

JEREMIAH 31:33

Contents

Introduction

In an essay written near the end of his life, French artist Henri Matisse shared some valuable insights he'd gained over the course of his long and prolific career. When it comes to creative endeavors, vision is paramount, and Matisse had learned that there is more to seeing clearly than what first meets the eye. "Everything that we see in our daily life is more or less distorted by acquired habits," he observed, and "something very like courage" is required to overcome those distortions. Reflecting on a lifetime of artistic challenges, he illustrated his point with this lovely example: "Nothing," he wrote, "is more difficult for a true painter than to paint a rose, because, before he can do so, he has first to forget all the roses that were ever painted."[1]

Our divine DNA includes the inheritance of creative artistry. In a wide assortment of ways, we are capable of expansive thought. And we naturally bring our own background to each subject we approach, especially those that are familiar. Preconceived notions and prior experiences shape our expectations and influence how we understand and make meaning from them. Even the most sincere mentor can inadvertently instill sticky ideas that may obscure or limit our vision. When a well-meaning teacher offers their understanding of a certain religious symbol, an impressionable student might accept that as the only "right" interpretation, rather than recognizing it as one of many. Sometimes it helps to back up a bit and approach a subject from a slightly different angle to find a new vantage point. A fresh perspective can reveal additional layers of meaning and insights well worth exploring.

Each summer, the walkway leading up to my local temple is lined with vibrant pink rose bushes in full bloom. I'd been passing them as I approached the temple doors for years, but it wasn't until the day my son and his fiancée posed for their wedding photos near them that I really *saw* them. Watching the talented photographer carefully consider how to best capture the beauty of that occasion with the help of those gorgeous roses provided me with a new perspective. Now, regardless of the season, I often pause as I approach the temple to appreciate the current stage of those rose bushes and anticipate their blossoms.

Figuratively, there are countless ways we might approach the house of the Lord—some shaped by prior experiences there, others influenced by thoughts parents, teachers, or friends have shared, and yet others curiously formed by speculative anticipation. Additionally, our personal worldview might predispose us to focus our attention on various elements of the temple experience more than others. Each approach acts as an interpretive lens, whether we realize it or not. What Matisse was suggesting is that we might intentionally, even bravely, choose to try on a new pair of glasses—new frames with different lenses through which to take a fresh look.

I'd like to invite you to join me in putting on some specific glasses as we approach the temple together in the coming pages. These lenses are specially honed to focus on developing a loving relationship with the Lord. As I've grown accustomed to wearing them, I've been amazed by how clearly I can now see God's love when I look at the ordinances and covenants of the temple. For me, that sharpened vision has proven personally powerful since, like Sister Tracy Y. Browning explained, Jesus Christ is "the purpose of our focus," and when we "see our lives *through Him*, [we] see *more of Him* in our lives."[2]

What I've discovered for myself is that approaching the temple with my eyes, ears, heart, and mind focused on Christ's covenant way of living and loving has changed how I approach my life. Temple worship has become more than an occasional opportunity to recalibrate my eternal perspective amid mortality's messy middle; it also creates space to practice the eternal principles of divine relationships that are gradually transforming me and my earthly relationships with those I love.

In the pages that follow, we will look expansively at the Christ-like characteristics we learn to love and emulate as we worship in His holy house. The first half of this book offers a supportive scaffolding that outlines the stretching process of mortality; chapters one through four focus on the journey of feeling, building, becoming, and sharing our lives with the Lord. An interlude transitions us into the second half, solidifying our understanding of the dynamic role of our bodies and spirits in helping us become like God as we embrace five covenant commitments to build loving relationships: obedience, sacrifice, the gospel, chastity, and consecration. Chapters five through nine will focus on these five covenants and help us see the various ways Christ lived these eternal principles of covenant relationships, teaching us, through His words and actions, His way of loving Heavenly Father and others. We will conclude with chapter ten, wrapping our entire eternal plan of progression in the arms of the Lord's atoning love.

The gospel of Jesus Christ is a gospel of love because *God is love* (see 1 John 4:7–8). His holy house is mortality's sacred space where we receive specialized instruction on *how* to love as He loves—not just in the distant eternities but right here, right now. We enter the temple to make covenants, we leave it to live them.[3] Divine love, grounded in core eternal principles, will bless *every* relationship, now and forever. As "The Living Christ" so beautifully concludes, "His way is the path that leads to happiness in this life *and* eternal life in the world to come."[4] As we approach His ways and His house together, I invite you to see the boundless ways His love can bless your life.

CHAPTER 1

Feeling at Home in the House of the Lord

What makes a house a home? Though it may seem cliche, *home is where the heart is.* We can personalize our own descriptions of what constitutes a loving home by adding our favorite adjectives, like tender, gentle, generous, warm. The list could go on and on as we flesh out the feelings and emotions of home. Let's paint a bigger picture of that precious sense of heartfelt belonging that humans crave.

If we could cozy up in front of a fire and share our favorite memories of the nostalgic smells, sounds, and sights that have become our unique beacons of love and belonging, a common feeling might emerge: comfort. Those physical, sensory-infused evidences of security in a place that feels familiar, safe, and comfortable sink in deep and stay with us.

Such lasting memories suggest that an ideal starting point for approaching the house of the Lord is recognizing it as a place of love and belonging. Since we might be less familiar with some elements of temple worship, having these two footings firmly in place will provide a secure base on which we can build. Let's turn to scripture to try to better understand how the Lord loves us.

In his letter to the Romans, the Apostle Paul captured the intense depth and reach of the Lord's relentless love for each of us by posing two poignant questions: "Who shall separate us from the love of Christ? Shall tribulation, or distress, or persecution, or famine, or nakedness, or peril, or sword?" (Romans 8:35). His answer is powerful as he passionately testifies based on his own experiences: "Nay. . . . Neither death, nor life, nor angels, nor principalities, nor powers, nor things present, nor things to come, nor height, nor depth, nor any other creature, shall be able to separate us from the love of God, which is in Christ Jesus our Lord" (Romans 8:37–39).

Expounding on God's love for us, President Thomas S. Monson echoed Paul's assuredness, declaring, "Your Heavenly Father loves you—each of you. That love never changes. It is not influenced by your appearance, by your possessions, or by the amount of money you have in your bank account. It is not changed by your talents and abilities. It is simply there. It is there for you when you are sad or happy, discouraged or hopeful. God's love is there for you whether or not you feel you deserve love. It is simply always there."[1]

I hope you've had personal experience with love like that; perhaps you remember a family member, friend, mentor, or teacher who loved you whether you were happy or sad, mad or glad. For me, that person was my grandmother. Instead of pointing out my deficiencies, she highlighted my strengths.[2] When I spent time with her, I was always better for it; I'd leave her presence as the best version of myself.

That kind of relationship is fueled by the type of love President M. Russell Ballard was describing when he noted that, ideally, "It is within our families that we learn unconditional love, which can come to us and draw us very close to God's love."[3] While our families may strive and struggle to reach this ideal, each does so uniquely, with various degrees of success and satisfaction.

It's reassuring to remember what Sister Tamara W. Runia pointed out. "In a fallen world there's no way to be a perfect spouse, parent, son or daughter, grandchild, mentor, or friend—but a million ways to be a good one."[4] Though no family is perfect, the family structure was designed to provide both a place to practice loving well *and* a place to feel safety, peace, and rest.

In the Old Testament, the Hebrew word frequently translated as "rest" (*menuhah*) tries to capture this "deep sense of belonging, of security."[5] For example, in Deuteronomy 12:9, as the Lord is teaching the children of Israel about the blessings that will flow from their covenant relationship with Him, He describes the "rest" that will accompany their "inheritance." Bible scholar Ellen Davis describes this kind of rest as "the unshakable assurance that a person or a people feels in the presence of God, even when enemies threaten." She goes on to describe this kind of peace as "the blessing of God's favor and continual presence, which gives freedom from the sources of deepest anxiety."[6]

That description dovetails beautifully with President Dallin H. Oaks' definition of *abide*, another word frequently used in scriptures to characterize that sense of feeling at home. He defines it as "a secure placement."[7] As the lyrics of the pleading hymn "Abide with Me!" longingly express, "When other helpers fail and comforts flee, Help of the helpless, oh, abide with me!"[8] It's therefore fitting that *abide* is so closely related to the word *abode*, a synonym for house or home.[9] When we feel at home in a place, we feel a deep sense of security and belonging based on unchangeable, unshakable, inseparable love—the kind of love God has for each of us.

This connection informs how it is equally accurate to say you feel "at home" in a *place* as it is to say you feel "at home" with a *person*. That sense of comfort is a function of both being in your grandmother's house *and* being with your grandmother. Though I can close my eyes and easily recall the smell of my grandmother's kitchen, that spicy-sweet scent reminds me more of her than of her oatmeal raisin cookies. That's because those tender feelings are all about our relationship—they stem from the fact that she is my grandmother, and I am her grandchild.

Relationships are the primary source of our secure sense of love and belonging. Our layers of identity generally derive from our relationships; they remind us of both *who* we are and *whose* we are. That's why understanding our divine identity and our inherent relationship with the Lord is so crucial to feeling at home in His holy house. As President Russell M. Nelson has testified, "In all of eternity, no one will ever know you or care about you more than He does. No one will ever be closer to you than He is."[10] President Nelson has repeatedly urged us to "know the truth about who [we] are. . . . [We] are literally spirit children of God."[11] While it's certainly true that we have many layers of identity, some of which come and go over time, no characteristic matters to the degree that our divine heritage does. None offers us such a clear vision of who we can ultimately become. God longs to give us "glimpses of who [we] may become."[12] Once we gain our own witness of this glorious truth, and then begin to familiarize ourselves with His sacred house, we naturally begin to feel at home there because we long to be *with Him.*

In addition to providing divine guidance and direction individually, our loving relationship with the Lord also has the power to bless all our other relationships as well. One of the benefits of spending time with my grandmother was that with each visit I gradually became more like her. Her kindness was contagious; she showed me what generous, unconditional love felt like, and the more deeply I felt it, the more I desired it, and longed to share those feelings with others that I loved. Time spent with the Lord, especially in His holy house, can do the same.

Just as my grandmother was the heart of her home, the Lord Jesus Christ is "the beating heart of the eternal gospel,"[13] and the love and belonging we are invited to feel in His house flows from our most sacred relationships—"the love of Heavenly Parents, the atoning gift of a divine Son, [and] the comforting guidance of the Holy Ghost"[14]—and from there into all of our other relationships. As President Jeffrey R. Holland put it, like so much of life, our temple experience "will mean little or nothing unless we find Jesus at the center of it all."[15] Home is, indeed, where the Heart is.

CHAPTER 2

Building on the Rock

A single symbol may have many multilayered meanings, which is why symbols are so valuable in fostering expansive thinking and learning. The simplest symbols, such as water or bread, can be the most thought-provoking. Though rocks or stones may represent various ideas or concepts throughout the scriptures, they are frequently used as symbols of Jesus Christ. In the standard works, Jesus Christ is variously described as "the Rock of Israel" (2 Samuel 23:3),[1] "the rock of thy strength" (Isaiah 17:10), "the rock of my salvation" (2 Nephi 4:30),[2] and "the Rock of Heaven" (Moses 7:53). These many examples repeatedly convey the sense of a rock upon which *to build*, as memorably emphasized in Helaman's plea to his sons: "Remember, remember that it is upon the rock of our Redeemer, who is Christ, the Son of God, that ye must build your foundation; . . . a sure foundation, a foundation whereon if men build they cannot fall" (Helaman 5:12).

This image of Christ as the rock upon which we must build our spiritual foundation is particularly fitting regarding the temple because Christ and His atoning love and sacrifice undergird *everything* we do there.[3] "Everything taught in the temple," emphasized President Russell M. Nelson, "increases our understanding of Jesus Christ."[4] From the praise we offer to the principles we learn, from the service we render to the peace we feel, our time with the Lord in His holy house naturally nurtures our relationship with Him.

Additionally, *ROCK* offers an ideal acronym to explore the eternally significant and sacred rites and privileges that we are invited to participate in within that sacred space. These four elements of eternity—Relationships, Ordinances, Covenants, and Knowledge—serve as basic building blocks to increase our understanding of the Savior's love and the godly power available to us in the house of the Lord.

Everything in the temple is securely built upon the Rock of our Salvation, our Savior, Jesus Christ. "Truly He loves us," Elder D. Todd Christofferson testified, "and because He loves us, He neither compels nor abandons us. Rather, He helps and guides us."[5] That help and guidance is God's gift of grace, firmly rooted in His ever-present love. *Grace* has been simply defined as "God's offer of relational love,"[6] His invitation into covenant relationship. Our covenantal ties to Christ, which we often collectively refer to as "the new and everlasting covenant," mean that by living *His way,* we can become *like Him.*[7] That's an extremely big idea—an *eternally* big idea. In fact, we might say that *grace* is Christ beckoning us to live and love like Him and with Him. *Everything* about the temple points to God's grace.

President Nelson described the unique, eternal nature of covenant relationship profoundly. He taught, "Making a covenant with God changes our relationship with Him forever. It blesses us with an extra measure of love and mercy. It affects who we are and how God will help us become what we can become."[8] Our temple worship—everything we feel and experience and practice in the house of the Lord—can be transformative because of the power inherent in our covenant relationship with Christ. And that is a relationship built on love.

Our secure, loving attachment to Him will help us examine the O and C of our acronym—ordinances and covenants—the dynamic duo of spiritual commitment. Simply defined, a covenant is an empowering promise, and an ordinance is its sacred physical representation. They are typically paired and powerfully complementary, as we will see with the salvific ordinances and covenants that are offered and administered in the temple. They include the ordinances of baptism and confirmation, Melchizedek priesthood ordination for men, receiving the endowment, and the sealing of husband and wife, with each of their associated covenant commitments. We call these ordinances and covenants "salvific" because they are required steps of progression along the path to salvation and exaltation. And because of their eternal necessity, each of these is offered by proxy in the house of the Lord so that no essential blessing is withheld from any child of God who chooses to participate in His great plan of progression.

Ordinances are divinely designed to require us to participate in a physical act of agency to signify our sincere desire to enter into covenant relationship with God. We must demonstrate, *by intentional, bodily action*, our choice to engage. This is one of the reasons our bodies are so valuable: with them, we are able to publicly manifest our reception of God's gracious invitation into covenant relationship with Him. No one "accidentally" gets baptized or endowed; covenants are far too significant for any sort of carelessness. Elder D. Todd Christofferson highlighted this crucial role of agency when he taught that "God will not act to make us something we do not choose by our actions to become."[9]

The Church of Jesus Christ of Latter-day Saints has a profoundly beautiful doctrine of embodiment; *we honor our bodies.*

We cherish the opportunity to learn and grow through them, and we look forward to eventually being reunited with them in the life to come. Our bodies quite literally facilitate agency; thanks to them, we can *choose* to participate in God's great work, and, in doing so, offer tangible evidence of that choice, which then serves as a personal guidepost along our covenant path.

Ordinances invite physical action, and their embodied nature acknowledges and honors our physical bodies as a crucial component of our eternal soul. President Nelson emphasized this, noting that we are "dual beings" comprised of body and spirit, "both of which emanate from God" and which combine to become "a living soul of supernal worth."[10] Our bodies matter. That doctrinal understanding and the accompanying respect for our bodies that it instills can help us live and lean into the covenant commitments that these ordinances represent and signify.

Additionally, our bodies are perhaps our most valuable learning tool. The five senses can be some of our very best teachers by creating precious and visceral memories. Seeing the beauty of a blooming rose, hearing the cry of a newborn baby, smelling the scent of fresh ocean air, tasting the tang of a juicy lime, or holding the hand of a hurting loved one opens our heart so the Spirit can rush in and fill its cracks and crevices with light and truth. Sight, sound, smell, taste, and touch all foster further understanding; each helps us feel God's love and sense the Spirit's guidance in practical and profound ways.

Let's take a deep dive into the ordinance of baptism and consider how we might learn by physically participating with its tangible elements. First and foremost, imagine the water in which we are immersed. We know from our experience that water is wet, but also that it can be cleansing and thirst quenching. Furthermore, its liquid state allows it not only to saturate but to infiltrate—it reaches into every nook and cranny, leaving nothing untouched or unchanged. Depending on one's circumstances, water can be deadly or lifesaving. In that sense, we might reflect on the countless water stories in scripture, including Noah's family and the flood (see Genesis 7–8), the children of Israel and the parting of the sea (see Exodus 14), the woman at the well (see John 4:5–30), and Jared and his extended family traveling in light-filled, tight-like-a-dish vessels (see Ether 6). Weaving our experiences together with theirs offers all sorts of insightful and expansive ways we might see the sacred symbolism of baptismal water.

Next, let's look at the clothing worn into the font. Both the person being baptized and the person doing the baptizing are dressed completely in white, which represents purity and the Holy Ghost (the color is linked to the Spirit by the dove associated with Noah's covenantal deliverance[11] and Jesus's own baptism).[12] We might also note that both participants enter the font shoeless, reminiscent of Moses being directed to remove his sandals before approaching the holy ground of the burning bush (see Exodus 3:5). Notice how something as seemingly routine as clothing can provide additional, thought-provoking insights, thanks to the physical elements of sacred ordinances that offer familiar connection points between earth and heaven, mortality and eternity.[13]

Finally, consider the posture and gestures of the baptismal ordinance. After entering the water together, the one being baptized holds firmly to the arm of the one doing the baptizing. The baptizee bravely submits to the baptizer, trusting that being immersed below the water comes with the assurance of being lifted back up again. It's a uniquely vulnerable position to voluntarily put yourself in—perhaps frightening, potentially dangerous, yet ultimately lifesaving.

The familiar, earthbound symbols of baptism can be mined endlessly for deeper meanings. This primary ordinance at once signifies spiritual cleansing, death and rebirth, and submission and trust; it's a sacred experience with Divinity, and all those layers of significance are evident without even examining the language of the ordinance.[14] Those words succinctly speak to these very concepts by focusing on the power and authority of the Godhead, delegated to those authorized to administer on their behalf, to welcome a person into a new level of relationship with God.

The process of confirmation, through which one receives the immeasurable gift of the Holy Ghost, initiates the potential for the Spirit's constant, guiding, and comforting companionship. As ordained priesthood holders place their hands on the recipient's head, those hands serve as a tangible conduit through which the Spirit's loving power flows. That covenant relationship will henceforth be characterized by striving for purity, seeking the sacred, and submitting to the Lord's will, all with the invaluable help of the Holy Spirit. Baptism is an encapsulated, one-time event recorded in heaven that marks an ongoing transformation that will continue for the rest of that person's life.

That continuing development is, quite literally, "brought to life" through the complementary nature of an ordinance's accompanying covenant(s). In this case, though *the ordinance* of baptism represents a singular moment in time, *the covenant commitment* that accompanies it—namely our promise to serve God, keep His commandments, and be willing to take upon ourselves the name of Jesus Christ—is a lifelong undertaking. The long-term project of covenant commitment follows a familiar, three-step model; first, we grow and change gradually and incrementally; second, we build on our experience, increased understanding, and maturity; and third, we are transformed because as we come to know better, we can begin to do better.[15] In a word, it is conversion, and conversion is deep knowledge acquisition.

In 2007, Elder David A. Bednar memorably likened the conversion process to pickling—transforming garden-grown cucumbers into pickles. In his conference address titled "Ye Must Be Born Again," he cleverly drew noteworthy connections between the *experience* of baptism and confirmation and the *way* of conversion, particularly noting that "steady, sustained, and complete immersion is required for the desired change to occur."[16] The spiritual rebirth symbolized by the act of baptism in fact occurs "gradually, almost imperceptibly, [as] our motives, our thoughts, our words, and our deeds become aligned with the will of God,"[17] facilitated by the companionship of the Holy Ghost. It's a process, informed by carefully articulated covenant commitments, that requires "time, persistence, and patience,"[18] though it's signified by a preliminary, one-time physical event.

Alma the Younger, sharing his own conversion story, testified that "all nations, kindreds, tongues and people, must be born again; yea, born of God, changed from their carnal and fallen state, to a state of righteousness, being redeemed of God, becoming his sons and his daughters; and thus they become new creatures; and unless they do this, they can in nowise inherit the kingdom of God" (Mosiah 27:25–26). Reflecting the complementing qualities of paired ordinances and covenants, Alma highlights the necessity of this crucial change while respecting its ongoing nature.

Becoming requires prolonged commitment. As Elder Bednar described, "Sporadic and shallow dipping in the doctrine of Christ and partial participation in His restored Church cannot produce the spiritual transformation that enables us to walk in a newness of life. Rather, fidelity to covenants, constancy of commitment, and offering our whole soul unto God are required if we are to receive the blessings of eternity."[19]

The conversion process is like any other kind of learning, but with amplified depth and significance since this is learning about God. Our faithful actions toward Him solidify our understanding of His unfailing fidelity for each of us. As Elder Patrick Kearon movingly testified, "God is in relentless pursuit" of each of us and "He employs every possible measure" to bring us home.[20] As we steadily strive to cultivate habits of daily discipleship, we come to know, see, and feel the goodness of the Lord through His personal presence in our lives. Our closer relationship with Him, through the sacred ordinances and our associated covenant commitments, gives us meaningful, firsthand knowledge of God's compassion, and the Holy Ghost adds to that knowledge by generously providing additional light.[21] We become like Him by living and loving His way, which allows us to progressively learn to see Him as He truly is (see Moroni 7:48). The Lord revealed to the Prophet Joseph, "Whatever principle of intelligence we attain unto in this life, it will rise with us in the resurrection" (Doctrine and Covenants 130:18). No knowledge is more valuable and impactful than a true understanding of the power of His infinite love for each of us.

CHAPTER 3

Becoming Bilingual

"Aimer, c'est agir." *To love is to act.* With these simple words, the great French writer Victor Hugo immortalized his life philosophy just days before he passed away.[1] He had lived a long, active life, which he spent loving God, freedom, and humanity, especially the marginalized. He spent his time in pursuit of the ideal balance between law and love, two of the most powerful languages of human experience. He cherished liberty because it provides the opportunity to assume personal responsibility and act courageously, as guided by the heart.

Love's defining characteristic is that it is freely given. It cannot be coerced; the moment it is, it ceases to be love. That's what makes love so immensely powerful—it is *always* a choice. Therefore, a grand plan of love *must* be built on moral agency—the ability to choose and to act according to one's own choice.[2] It follows, then, that in God's great plan of love, which we call *exaltation*, agency is not secondary, nor is it an end in itself; rather, it is of primary importance because it is the means to the end. We commit to love God and to love one another and to make that choice evident through our actions.

Agency has been described in many memorable ways as prophets, leaders, and great thinkers have tried to capture its magnitude in the eternal scheme of things. President David O. McKay called it "God's greatest gift to man,"[3] and his successor Joseph Fielding Smith added that it is "the only principle upon which exaltation can come."[4] Elder Dale G. and Sister Ruth L. Renlund named agency "the eternal principle of progression,"[5] and Elder George Q. Morris said it is "the very essence of our existence."[6] Theologian-philosopher C. S. Lewis defined it through the lens of love, declaring it to be "the only thing that makes possible any love or goodness or joy worth having," since God's divine design is "the happiness of being freely, voluntarily united to Him and to each other." Then, as if finishing the perfect mathematical proof, Mr. Lewis concluded, "and for that [His children] must be free."[7]

All that to say that we offer evidence of our love by our self-willed actions. But the curious thing about love and agency is that they work together in a mutually reinforcing way: when we act *toward* love, our movement in that direction acts on us; in other words, our actions can shape and form our love. That's why it's possible, over time, to intentionally replace poor habits with better ones. Human nature is designed so that as our love guides our actions, our actions grow our love. This virtuous cycle highlights the immense power of participation.[8]

This is the kind of growth and transformation that love so gently invites. It is how we deepen a relationship: one loving act at a time. If celestial life is a way of living and loving, then we may begin that celestializing process here and now by intentionally living and loving *that way* here and now. And in the temple, the Lord is inviting us to do exactly that. Through our willing participation, we may gradually become what we hope to someday be.

So, one might fairly ask, "If everything in the temple speaks to love and agency, why do we call the five covenants of the endowment 'laws?'" In this modern world, rules and regulations feel contrary to the language of love; they sound more like the language of law. How can we reconcile these two distinct dialects?

The first thing to consider is that there are different *kinds* of laws. Some laws are practical, like "rules of the road," because they help people cooperate. For example, in the United States, people drive on the right side of the road, but if one did that in England, it would be quite problematic. Neither side is inherently better; what matters is that everyone in the community agrees on which they choose.

Other laws are what we might call "moral imperatives" because they reflect moral relativism; those can shift given changing social norms or the current political climate. In the 1960s, cigarette ads glamorized smoking in ways that were especially appealing to young people, and they were everywhere—on billboards, magazines, and television. Today, with better medical understanding, targeting children and teens with such a dangerous drug is widely prohibited. Surprisingly, though, the same does not hold true for the alcohol industry, though science has likewise revealed alcohol consumption to be a highly risky business.

Then there's a third kind of law—a kind that doesn't change according to trends or politics or location—*natural laws*, such as gravity. We couldn't "break" the law of gravity if we tried because it's simply *the way things work.* Natural laws are sure and constant, predictable and dependable. Rather than denying them, we study to understand them, so we can learn to work with them, like scientists and athletes do. Understanding gravity can actually help a baseball player throw a ball farther or a ballerina turn a pirouette faster.

So yes, scripture and the sacred language of the temple (what might be called *liturgy*[9]) often use the judicial-sounding language of law, but typically in the sense of natural, *eternal* law. This language has everything to do with divine love. These are agency-honoring laws because they are clearly defined and completely transparent; they are the very opposite of arbitrary, capricious, or restrictive.[10] They are constant and predictable. They are liberating, not limiting, because they provide parameters within which we can learn to freely function.[11] President Russell M. Nelson called such divine laws "incontrovertible" and "absolute truth," noting that "eternal laws operate in and affect each of our lives, whether we believe in them or not."[12] In fact, agency itself has been described using the dependable language of eternal law. Elder Boyd K. Packer called it "the very law essential to the plan,"[13] and Elder Tad R. Callister described it as "the keystone upon which heaven and earth are governed."[14]

If all this feels a bit confusing, consider how you may have grown up talking about the law of the fast and the law of tithing. How has your understanding of these laws evolved and expanded over the years? Ideally, personal experience helps us see both as powerful gifts: when we abide by these laws, we are richly blessed. Yet we're also taught that fasting involves skipping two meals and tithing means giving ten percent, and those sound a lot like arbitrary rules. But there's an important interplay between principles and guidelines that we might not fully appreciate when we're young. The principle of fasting draws us closer to God as our physical hunger directs our attention to a deep need, causing us to turn to Him for spiritual fulfillment. The guidelines are meant to guide our practice: they help us willingly wait in that yearning space and demonstrate our trust in Him through our agency, which expands our love and strengthens our relationship, as He simultaneously fills our void.

Likewise, the principle of tithing is grounded in the divine truth that by gratefully acknowledging God's loving generosity and abundance, and willingly giving a portion back to Him, He can do more with the remainder than we could do with the entirety. The ten percent guideline invites us to demonstrate our trust in His providence while respecting our agency, growing our love, and deepening our relationship with Him.

Similarly, in the temple we are invited to dedicate ourselves to five eternal principles of covenant relationship, and we call these "laws" as well: the law of obedience, the law of sacrifice, the law of the gospel of Jesus Christ, the law of chastity, and the law of consecration. These are the five specific covenants we make as we receive the endowment.[15] And as eternal laws, our success and happiness depend on our understanding and working with them.[16]

Like all divine laws, they're immune from moral relativism—they won't change based on cultural trends or popular vote—and they are only secondarily about rules and guidelines. Though eternal truths are constant, the *words* through which we understand them may not be, since language lives in mortal constructs and shifts among cultures and contexts. Adjustments are occasionally made by prophets to reach and relate to a growing, global faith family. As President Nelson has explained, these helpful changes are "evidence that the Lord is actively directing His Church,"[17] valuable reminders of the ongoing restoration. The Lord wants us to understand our covenants with Him.[18]

First and foremost, God's laws are fundamental to the wise use of trust and power, in both our relationship with God and our relationships with others. These covenants mark the way to lasting happiness because they are *God's way of living and loving.* Studying, understanding, and embracing them is transformative because when we live His Way, we can become like Him.[19]

In this sense, adopting some new wording of our own might

help us interpret our relationship with God more expansively. For example, in English, it feels slightly awkward to speak of "keeping" these eternally true principles since, in the same sense that gravity is "true," they are intended as God's way of living, His method of *becoming*. The ancient Hebrew idea, articulated in the verb *shamar* (שָׁמַר), depicts this big idea. Though it is typically translated as "keep" and often interpreted as "obey," it can be more broadly thought of as to guard, protect, treasure, or cherish.[20] It's used in this sense in Exodus 19:5 when the Lord teaches Moses on Mount Sinai about the relationship He intends for covenant Israel. "Now therefore, if ye will obey my voice indeed, and *keep* my covenant, then ye shall be a peculiar treasure unto me above all people: for all the earth is mine" (emphasis added). *Shamar* reflects one's attitude or posture of embracing Christ's covenant way of living and loving.

Our Father in Heaven is completely invested in our happiness. His great plan is all about love. *Every* ordinance, covenant, and commandment is designed to promote happiness, goodness, and eternal glory. And not only *later,* but also *right now.* Elder Richard G. Scott rightly called this "the genius of the gospel plan," since "by doing, principally in selfless service to others, those things the Lord counsels us to do, we are given every understanding, every capacity, every capability necessary to provide rich fulfillment in this life and the preparation necessary for eternal happiness in the presence of the Father."[21] It's love and action, action and love, mutually reinforcing each other, lifting us upward.

God's love starts in our hearts and then radiates outward, strengthening and deepening all our relationships as we practice these eternal principles. Our covenant relationship with Him begins that transformative process, as the prophet Jeremiah expressed on the Lord's behalf. "This shall be the covenant that I will make with the house of Israel. . . . I will put my law in their inward parts, and write it in their hearts; and will be their God, and they shall be my people" (Jeremiah 31:33). Loving His law transforms our actions as we cherish His way of living and loving and emulate it; simultaneously, He grows our understanding, capacity, and capability. Through divine collaboration, we gather and build Zion.

One Evangelical scholar in the field of marriage and family relations explains the far-reaching power of love this way: "When I experience love, it influences all of [my] needs positively. I am now freed to develop my potential. I am more secure in my self-worth and can now turn my efforts outward instead of being obsessed with my own needs. True love always liberates."[22] His expert opinion highlights the crux of God's great plan of happiness, as described by President M. Russell Ballard: "True happiness depends upon our relationship with God, with Jesus Christ, and with each other."[23] Ordinances, covenants, and commandments are gifts given to facilitate and bless those sacred relationships. God longs to enlarge and expand our understanding, capacity, and capability for loving relations. Truly, divine law *is* divine love. It is perfect love, freely given.

CHAPTER 4

Sharing the Love and Sharing the Load

Learning to share is part of growing up. You may not remember your own early childhood, but if you've spent time with a three-year-old, you may have noticed that they're just barely capable of overriding their childlike tendency toward egocentrism and selfishness.[1] It may seem that two of their favorite words are "me" and "mine!" For children, and sometimes even adults, managing a healthy balance between autonomy and cooperation might take some guidance. Having a kind coach and, occasionally, a referee, helps. Still, this interplay may look more like taking turns than actual sharing. The shift to interdependent cooperation happens gradually; eventually, playmates start to feel like friends when their interactions become more like a metaphorical game of four-square.

In the more grown-up, Sunday sense, we talk about sharing our testimony in sacrament meeting, or sharing an experience during a lesson, both of which foster friendship via vulnerability. But relationships really begin to thrive when our sharing incorporates reciprocity—when there's a comfortable back-and-forth that draws us in and draws us close, as if we're being knitted together (see Mosiah 18:21).[2] That's *sharing* in the truest, most mature sense of the word. And like the versions of sharing that often precede it, it typically begins with a generous offer—a literal or figurative outstretched hand; then, in its reception and accompanying response, momentum builds, and the cycle continues. Friendship begins when a single, loving act is received, and it grows when that act is reciprocated.

That's also how our covenant relationship with the Lord is built. As the King James Version renders John's first letter, "We love him, because he first loved us" (1 John 4:19). Our receiving and then reciprocating that love naturally strengthens the relationship. In his Gospel, John highlights the impact of our response when he reminds us of Jesus's promise, "Abide in me, and I in you" (John 15:4). Rather than our love being a transaction (He loves us and so we love Him), it instead becomes a virtuous cycle—He loves us, which inspires us to love Him, which leads Him to love us, and so on. And the Prophet Joseph reiterated Christ's message in a rich, temple-related revelation, again relaying the Lord's generous invitation for deeper relationship: "Draw near unto me and I will draw near unto you" (Doctrine and Covenants 88:63).

In a powerful devotional address focused on how we build "stronger and closer connection to God," Elder Dale G. Renlund explained that "when we make a covenantal bond with God, we *share* a covenant with Him. We experience and participate *together* in the covenant."[3] Sister Kristen M. Yee of the General Relief Society Presidency, echoing Elder Renlund in a message just two days later, highlighted the virtuous upward cycle such sharing organically facilitates, testifying, "When we feel His love and reciprocate that love by choosing Him every day, the gospel becomes less about checkboxes and more about love and desire."[4] That's the beauty and power of covenant relationships built on and supported by God's perfect love: they are constructed of mutual commitment and shared purpose because they are a loving and collaborative *partnership*. Though the ordinances might resemble mile markers along the covenant path, our covenants are more representative of *the way* we walk that path, which is *with Jesus*. That idea is emphasized through one of Christ's sacred names, Emmanuel, which means *God with us*. The covenant way implies journeying *with* Him: taking His outstretched hand, embracing and practicing His way of walking, loving, and living as He directs and demonstrates.

That kind of flourishing friendship is what faith in Jesus Christ is all about. Like all good friendships, it depends on commitment and loyalty, and it deepens and strengthens through time spent together. And what better place to spend time together than in His holy house? That's where God's grace—His offer of relational love—is most generously given through the reinforcing layers of successive temple ordinances and covenants.[5]

The holy endowment, available only in the temple, is one of the greatest gifts God offers us—"literally a gift from God through which He blesses His children."[6] It is an invitation to participate intimately in God's way of living and loving. Scripture asks a valuable question: "For what doth it profit a man if a gift is bestowed upon him, and he receive not the gift?" Real-life experience bears witness to the answer that follows: "Behold, he rejoices not in that which is given unto him, neither rejoices in him who is the giver of the gift" (Doctrine and Covenants 88:33). When we reject a gift, we often inadvertently reject the giver. And the reverse is typically also true. Receiving a gift honors the giver. *Receive* is ordinance language that is familiar; when a person is confirmed, they are directed to "*receive* the Holy Ghost,"[7] and we refer to "*receiving* our own endowment." As one wise gospel scholar put it, "What we choose to embrace, to be responsive to, is the purest reflection of who we are and what we love."[8]

How we receive a gift sends a strong message. Most of us have felt that disappointment that follows a slightly hesitant, overly polite, "Thank you . . . It's just what I wanted." We instantly reconsider or second-guess our offering. But how differently we feel when we watch genuine enthusiasm spread across the recipient's face!

The Lord offers us an incredible gift of love in His holy house. It is a divine gift of heavenly knowledge, power, and direction that comes with increased hope, comfort, and peace.[9] Understandably, He wants there to be no confusion about the impact He intends this gift to have. Because of the magnitude of what He is offering, He wants there to be completely transparent qualifications associated with receiving a temple recommend.[10] Collectively, we refer to these qualifying standards as *temple worthiness*. These do not question your worth. It is not a question of whether or not God wants you in His temple. It is a question of whether you are currently willing and ready to embrace the obligations that accompany entering a deeper covenant relationship with the Lord.

Your *worth* is infinite because you are a child of God who loves you perfectly and completely. As President Spencer W. Kimball declared: "God is your Father. He loves you. He and your Mother in heaven value you beyond any measure. . . . You are unique. One of a kind, made of the eternal intelligence which gives you claim upon eternal life. Let there be no question in your mind about your value as an individual. The whole intent of the gospel plan is to provide an opportunity for each of you to reach your fullest potential, which is eternal progression and the possibility of godhood."[11]

Your *divine worth* is indisputable! President Joy D. Jones reiterated that, explaining that "our worth was determined before we ever came to this earth," and then, for emphasis, she added, "*no matter what*, we *always* have worth in the eyes of our Heavenly

Father."[12] Our worth is completely independent of our current actions or attitudes, as President Thomas S. Monson noted, saying, "God's love is there for you whether or not you feel you deserve love. It is simply *always* there."[13] Heavenly Father oversaw the Creation of the earth "for the express purpose of providing an opportunity for you and for me to have the stretching and refining experiences of mortality, the chance to use our God-given moral agency to choose Him" and "to one day return home to Him."[14] You are, quite literally, His work and His glory (see Moses 1:39). Because you are His child, there is no question of your infinite worth; God is reaching out to you constantly, offering His divine love and assistance.

Your *worthiness,* on the other hand, asks if *you* are reaching out toward *Him.* Worthiness is about your current trending direction; it asks if you are *striving.*[15] Importantly, it does *not* ask if you are *perfect.* Former Brigham Young University President Cecil O. Samuelson clearly clarified that common confusion during a campus devotional, emphatically declaring, "One can be fully worthy in a gospel sense and yet still be growing while dealing with personal imperfections."[16] It is completely erroneous to equate gospel *worthiness* with mortal *perfection.* As President Russell M. Nelson so succinctly stated, "Perfection is pending."[17] He carefully explained that Christ's direction that we be "perfect, even as [our] Father in heaven is perfect" (Matthew 5:48) comes from the Greek *teleios,* meaning "complete," closely related to *telos* ("end") and *teleiono* ("to reach a distant end, to be fully developed, to finish").[18] *Tele-* is a prefix we know well, thanks to *tele*phone and *tele*vision. Each use describes distance, literally "distant sound" and "distant vision," respectively. As the prophet lovingly reiterated, *perfect* does not imply "'freedom from 'error'; it implies 'achieving a *distant* objective.'"[19]

The opportunity to prepare and qualify to receive our endowment and thereby foster a deeper relationship with the Lord is a generous offer that allows us to practice patterns of commitment and growth that we will later enter into more formally. This qualifying process demonstrates great love and respects our agency. We are being invited by God to provide clear evidence of our sincere desire to participate in divine partnership.

Alma highlighted this kind of faithful desire when he described how his people received God's offer of baptism, the first layer of covenant commitment. When asking if they desired a closer relationship with Christ—"to come into the fold of God, and to be called his people"—he clearly explained what such a commitment would entail: They would demonstrate their devotion by living and loving *His way*, including bearing one another's burdens, mourning with one another, and comforting one another; in short, standing as witnesses of God in every possible way.[20] After delineating what divine partnership looks like, he again asked if this was what they desired. Celebrating both Alma's transparency and God's gracious gift, "they clapped their hands for joy," exclaiming, "This is the desire of our hearts" (Mosiah 18:8–11).

Covenant relationship has often been compared to a yoke, a rich and multivalent symbol. According to the Anchor Bible Dictionary, "In the earliest periods the yoke was the simple instrument which bound animals—singularly, in pair, or in groups—to a mechanism of production."[21] In an agricultural society like ancient Israel, this was a familiar device that naturally evolved to symbolize "the owner-owned, master-slave, lord-subject relationship," designating not only submission but belonging.[22] A yoke was recognized as "the outward sign of an inward relationship."[23]

In a deeply symbolic sense, wearing a yoke, like being branded or marked, implied cooperation and obedience to one's master.

Covenants, like yokes, make partnership possible. The Savior Himself invites us to take His yoke upon us, "even though," as Elder David A. Bednar has noted, "our best efforts are not equal to and cannot be compared with His."[24] Carrying a load is not only easier when done with Him, in many crucial cases, it is *only* done with Him. Ultimately, it is only by humbly and submissively choosing to wear His yoke that we are able to accomplish the eternal tasks set before us. Exaltation must be completed in partnership—we cannot reach our desired destination on our own, nor can He do the work of getting us there without our active and willing participation. It is a joint effort, dependent on covenant relationship. Putting on His yoke and submitting to His will is how we access His power.

Anciently, the prophet Nephi spoke of accessing God's power through covenant relationship. In his great vision of the tree of life, he describes how "the power of the Lamb of God" descended upon "the covenant people of the Lord," arming them "with the power of God in great glory" (1 Nephi 14:14).[25]

More recently, President Russell M. Nelson has testified of this same crucial truth. He taught that "every woman and every man who makes covenants with God and keeps those covenants" is blessed with "direct access to the power of God." Furthermore, "Those who are endowed in the house of the Lord receive a gift of God's priesthood power by virtue of their covenant, along with a gift of knowledge to know how to draw upon that power."[26]

In a later address, he continued to urge us to take Christ's generously offered covenant yoke upon us, teaching, "As you come unto Him in faith, He will guide, preserve, and protect you. He will heal your broken heart and comfort you in your distress, He will give you access to His power. And He will make the impossible in your life become possible."[27]

In other words, though God's love is certain, access to His power is not. We access His power and thereby grow our capacity when we partner with Him, humbly and submissively choosing to enter into covenant relationship, and we signify that choice by participating in the ordinances of the priesthood offered within His holy house. In doing so, we actively, physically, and personally demonstrate our sincere desire to reach up and take His offered hand. It is by receiving the gift of our covenants that we are able to truly share the love and share the load with our Savior Jesus Christ.

Interlude

Let's begin our look at the five core covenants of the temple endowment by briefly examining some illuminating word origins. The root *tem-* means "to cut."[1] Therefore, a *temple* is a place "cut out," reserved, or set apart, for worship. Interestingly, the ancient Israelites referred to making a covenant as "cutting" a covenant.[2]

The temple is also a place to *contemplate*, or to slow down and ponder more deeply. In this sense, contemplation implies setting apart a space for observation, particularly for spiritual musings. Over time, *contemplation* absorbed the additional nuance of holding an idea continuously before the mind, as if one were holding up a *template* or pattern, two more derivatives of the root *tem*.

Examining this additional angle, we discover that *pattern* also corresponds to the French *patron*, meaning a protector or model. A patron safeguards, supports, and encourages,[3] reminding us that the temple, too, is meant to be a place of protection, support, and encouragement.

These converging ideas of *temple, contemplate, template, pattern,* and *patron* might inspire us to carve out time and space to slow down and ponder more deeply, directing our attention toward Christ—a Divine Original worthy of our devoted imitation.

Elder Robert D. Hales explained this Christocentric intersection perfectly, teaching that in the Lord's holy house we learn and "establish patterns of Christlike living. These include obedience, making sacrifices to keep the commandments, loving one another, being chaste in thought and action, and giving of ourselves to build the kingdom of God."[4] These five laws, which constitute Christ's covenant way of living and loving, are fundamental to our endowment because, as Elder Hales continued, "through the Savior's Atonement and by following these basic patterns of faithfulness, we receive 'power from on high' to face the challenges of life."[5] These multiple, successive covenants "are not only sequential but also additive and even synergistic,"[6] meaning that "each covenant adds a bond," as Elder Dale G. Renlund described, drawing us closer to God and strengthening our relationship with Him.[7] Each of the five reinforces the others, effectively helping us "mature in our discipleship."[8]

The Old Testament story of Rahab (Joshua 2) includes an intriguing symbol—a simple, red thread—that we can extract and examine more closely to illustrate this protective power of multiple covenant commitments. Doing so might help us approach the temple and the five covenants we enter into as we receive our own endowment there, with fresh eyes and expansive thinking.

Rahab was a savvy and courageous woman who played a pivotal role in the story of Covenant Israel. The book of Joshua tells the tale of two spies infiltrating the city of Jericho prior to attacking it under the command of Joshua.[9] Recognizing the dangerous situation her family faced with Joshua's formidable forces approaching, Rahab made the difficult decision to offer a hiding place to the Jewish spies in exchange for her family's safety and eventual deliverance. As part of the arrangement, she requested "a true token" (Joshua 2:12) from the two men as physical evidence of their agreement.[10] In response, the spies directed her to secure a "scarlet thread" (Joshua 2:18) in her window—the same window, built high into the city wall, through which she would help them escape with the use of a strong cord (Joshua 2:15). This visible thread would signify her special relationship with the children of Israel.

I sense a connection between the spies' strong cord and Rahab's red thread, which may be subtly woven into the Hebrew word *tikvah* (used for Rahab's scarlet thread in Joshua 2:18), a homonym that holds an interesting connotation: it can be concretely defined as "a cord" or "a rope," but it can be more abstractly defined as "hope."[11] This dual meaning hints at a metaphorical association between the strength of a multistrand rope and the faith-filled expectation of deliverance from imminent danger to secure safety, the kind we have through our covenant relationship with the Lord.[12]

In pondering the five covenants, some may wonder, "If we have already been baptized, why are additional covenants necessary?" I think the symbol of a rope highlights Elder Renlund's point: braiding a rope with multiple strands offers additional strength and therefore added security. As the sensible Preacher of Ecclesiastes wisely observes, "A threefold cord is not quickly broken" (Ecclesiastes 4:12). With every added strand, a rope becomes sturdier and more capable of doing its lifting, supporting, binding work. Additionally, the interweaving of the strands adds stability because it prevents unraveling, furthering its desired durability. Though some might like the idea of having "no strings attached," when the need for rescue arises, the more strings, the better![13] Each subsequent covenant connection we make with Christ lifts, supports, and binds us to His godly power and grace more securely.[14]

The *covenant path* is the phrase we commonly use to represent this sequential nature of covenant commitment.[15] More than a *road* marked by signposts, that term signifies a *way* of traveling, a way that becomes increasingly secure and empowering as we grow and progress. Elder Renlund described our covenants as "overlapping and mutually reinforcing," noting that it's how we are able to "mature in our discipleship."[16]

And that maturing discipleship has powerful repercussions, not just in the eternities, but here and now. Developing our covenant relationship with God elevates *all* of our relationships, as Sister Kristen M. Yee has taught, because Christ's covenant way of living and loving blesses us through God's grace. Because of His gracious love, He grants us the "strength and power to navigate and nurture our relationships with increased personal revelation, peace, and divine help."[17] It's as if the Lord is teaching us how to use our personal rope of hope to follow His example and lift and support each of our loved ones, binding them to us horizontally even as we are being bound to Him vertically.

Scholar Sam Brown summarized this way of seeing the additive power of each successive strand of our temple covenants in familiar, tangible terms when he wrote, "The temple tells a divine story about being entangled—entangled in a physical body and entangled in the lives of others. That entanglement, which shines brightly in the principles and ordinances of the gospel, is the great mystery of the universe, and it is our pathway to heaven."[18] The protective interweaving, made possible by our covenant relationship with Christ, is why the endowment—with its invitation to embrace and practice the five eternal principles of loving relationship—is such a powerful gift of grace that can transform every aspect of our lives.

Let's turn our attention now to those five life-changing principles—obedience, sacrifice, Christ's gospel, chastity, and consecration—and explore how they can improve and strengthen each of our interactions, both divine and mortal.

CHAPTER 5

The Way of Obedience

For centuries, sacred structures have featured "the architecture of ascension"— "a deliberate verticality which reaches toward heaven."[1] This design physically highlights a fundamental concept of the endowment, characterized by prophets as a "step-by-step ascent into the Eternal Presence."[2] Each additional step lifts us closer to God and strengthens our covenant relationship with Him.[3]

The pioneer-era Manti Utah Temple memorably illustrates this in its two towers' spiral staircases, renowned for their grandeur and expert craftsmanship.[4] With their six complete rotations and a vertical rise of over seventy-six feet, they are spectacular! Each upward step allows temple patrons to personally experience that metaphorical heavenward climb—a virtuous cycle of spiritual growth and maturity made possible by "a succession of right choices"[5]—our commitment to living Christ's covenant way.

A staircase is an ideal symbol for this grace-filled concept because it accommodates both ups and downs, as well as sideways movement. There's space to pause and rest, to let others pass, and to reach back to help a friend. And wide treads and sturdy handrails comfortably allow for a side-by-side climb. Christ's atoning love for us does the same. His grace provides room for each of us to move cooperatively at a unique pace and in an individual manner. The great plan of happiness allows for all of mortals' and mortality's variability. We can change direction, pause to catch our breath, and enjoy each other's camaraderie as we climb.[6]

Our ascent is fueled and reinforced by obedience, making way for "a future without limit" for each who faithfully embraces Christ's ways, as Elder Richard G. Scott said. He assured, "Your quiet, uncompromising determination to live a righteous life will couple you with inspiration and power beyond your imagination,"[7] thanks to God's grace. We might not always keep a steady pace, or even a constant direction, but our desire to climb and Christ's offer to assist us alchemize our limited ability into infinite capacity.

Elder D. Todd Christofferson expanded this idea, describing how "each new law or commandment we learn to live is like one more rung or step on a ladder that enables us to climb higher and higher."[8] Rather than feeling restrictive or limiting, he said, "those who *live the experience*—who give themselves freely and unreservedly to the covenant life—find greater liberty and fulfillment."[9] That coupling of our enthusiastic obedience paired with God's generous help energizes us, freeing us to keep climbing in loving partnership with the Lord.

In the Church, we formally define *obedience* as "striving to keep Heavenly Father's commandments,"[10] but we can easily recognize it by its commitment, dedication, and fidelity—the key components of *loyalty*. This is fitting since, as President Jeffrey R. Holland taught, "the crowning characteristic of love is always loyalty."[11] And Jesus Himself specified precisely what loyal love for Him should look like: "If ye love me, keep my commandments" (John 14:15). Obedience is fundamental to demonstrating our desire to love Him and live His way.

During His mortal life, Jesus exemplified obedience clearly and constantly, from the very first words Luke records Him speaking at the young age of twelve. When Mary and Joseph realize Jesus is missing from their group as they are traveling home from Jerusalem, they spend three anxious days searching for Him, finally finding Him in the temple. Expressing His surprise at their emotional pleas for an explanation, He responds, "How is it that ye sought me? Wist ye not that I must be about my Father's business?" (Luke 2:49). Even as a somewhat typical pre-teen, He was committed to being loyal to God's will.

As we strive to follow His example, our devotion initiates generative growth that Scottish mountaineer and war hero William Hutchinson Murray understood well. His harrowing experiences, from the peaks of the Alps to the depths of a German prisoner of war camp in World War II, taught him what he called "[the] one elementary truth," that "until one is *committed,* there is hesitancy, the chance to draw back, always ineffectiveness," but "the moment one definitely commits oneself, then Providence moves too."[12] That divine strength of covenant partnership helps us keep climbing.

Both love and obedience depend on agency, but being free to choose is only half of the story; the other half is dedication. We want to be free, but we want to be free to *do* something *worth doing.*[13] Elder Christofferson explained that "God gave [us] agency and Jesus showed [us] how to use it so that eventually [we] could learn what They know, do what They do, and be what They are."[14] In short, when we live Their way, we can become like Them. This divine truth is the essence of the new and everlasting covenant.[15] Choosing to be obedient to the Lord's counsel illustrates both that we trust that the direction comes from God *and* that living God's way matters to us.

In light of this truth, it's interesting to consider both ways we use the word *dedicate:* to stick with a particular pursuit and to make something sacred. Aren't they actually one and the same? As civic advocate Pete Davis says, "We do something holy in those few extraordinary moments when we make commitments. And we do something holy in those countless ordinary moments when we keep them."[16] The sacred work of embracing the Lord's covenant way of life changes us.

Our dedicated attention and sustained engagement are powerful tools for our progress because transformation happens slowly; *becoming* takes time. In the face of distractions, temptation, and fatigue, our very human efforts to stay attentive may falter, but cleaving to the Lord through our covenantal love helps us hang on when we might otherwise drift. Gratefully, God's merciful process and plan are designed to handle that divine tension between liberation and dedication perfectly.

The Lord's commandments and the constraints that naturally accompany them provide valuable parameters within which we can work. Author Willa Cather likened these blessings of boundaries to a frame, noting that "the first thing an artist does when he begins a new work is to lay down the barriers and limitations" because, without them, the possibilities are simply too vast to manage.[17] Though somewhat counterintuitive, dedicated space, clearly defined, actually fosters creativity.

Likening this concept to our covenants, Elder Christofferson explained that, rather than being confining, "obedience gives us greater control over our lives" because it increases our capacity "to work and create."[18] Commitment carves out the time and space that transformation and growth require.

Our long-term loyalty to God and His plan—even when it's hard—is the very essence of *faithfulness,* which, in certain contexts, is more commonly called *fidelity*. Fidelity strengthens every relationship because, in declaring our priorities, it promotes trust. "When we put God first," President Ezra Taft Benson taught, "all other things fall into their proper place or drop out of our lives. Our love of the Lord will govern the claims on our affections, the demands on our time, [and] the interests we pursue."[19] Seeing obedience through faith's frame of commitment, dedication, and fidelity reminds us that *what* matters most ought to be a function of *who* matters most.

Another crucial facet of faithful obedience is humility. Obedience is a choice, as we know, but as Elder L. Tom Perry pointed out, it often entails choosing between "our own limited knowledge and power and God's unlimited wisdom and omnipotence."[20] Humbly acknowledging the cavernous gap between the two, rather than leaning on our own understanding, causes us to pause and consider taking the bridge that spans it—and that bridge is obedience. As we trustingly venture onto it, it guides us to safe passage as things on the far side become clearer (Proverbs 3:5).

Each time we humbly step onto that bridge, trusting that it can support us, our relationship with the Lord grows stronger because we are moving closer to Him. One popular preacher recently put it this way: "Acts of obedience allow our faith to intersect with God's faithfulness. It is at that intersection that we see God work. And when we see Him work our faith gets bigger."[21] The law of obedience is an eternal law—as dependable as the laws of physics that govern bridge building and staircase construction; it has always been true, and it always will be because it is *the way things work.*

Centuries ago, another wise theologian, Thomas Aquinas, also recognized this enduring concept. In carefully studying the law, he began to see it more clearly, and he came to understand that it's a law made of love, built firmly on the Rock.[22] He thoughtfully recorded his findings, writing, "Keeping the commandments is not the cause of divine friendship but the sign, the sign both that God loves us and that we love God."[23] It all focuses on God's grace. Obedience is not about a contractual agreement, it's about a covenant relationship; God moves first, and we follow (see 1 John 4:19). This trusting approach to life, the way of obedience, encompasses countless Christlike attributes, including loyalty, commitment, dedication, fidelity, and humility; therefore, practicing, striving, and learning to live and love this way will naturally lift every relationship—our heavenly friendships as well as our earthly ones—eventually making them *all* divine.

CHAPTER 6

The Way of Sacrifice

"It was *so* worth it!" If you've ever said that, you have an inherent sense of sacrifice. You understand, from personal experience, that feeling that leads you to give up something good now for something better later. That now-and-later timeline can be short or long. For example, you might give up a few dollars for the immediate satisfaction of an ice cream cone, worth more to you than the spare change in your pocket. Or, on a larger scale, you might give up a few years of relative freedom to pursue higher education because you expect the eventual returns to be more fulfilling and satisfying than the benefits of sleeping in and bouncing between part-time jobs. Because of the finite nature of so many aspects of mortality—our time, our resources, and our energy—we make these kinds of decisions frequently, often without even realizing it and whether we physically signify them or not.

Value and investment are a few basic economic principles underlying our innate sense of what is "worth it." They speak to why we might choose to sacrifice. Something's *value* is equivalent to what you are willing to give up (or "pay," or "sacrifice") in exchange for it. And your decision to participate in that exchange reflects your belief that this *investment* will be beneficial; in other words, that its long-term value somehow exceeds its current cost.

Additionally, the length of time between the investment and its return reveals much about the power of the associated commitment. A nearly instantaneous exchange, like the ice cream cone, is often merely transactional, but a further-reaching return, like a college education, is actually transformational.

The only thing better than finding some*thing* worth sacrificing for is finding some*one*. And when we do, we naturally invest in the relationship through gifts and offerings. Academically, sociologists describe this relational economy of gift giving as "the means through which individuals communicate the values which they assign to their significant others."[1] In plain English, we call it "showing love." That's an interesting way to reframe sacrifice. People willingly sacrifice for those they love. You hopefully have personal evidence of this. Extrapolating the feelings related to gift giving and applying them to the gift of the temple endowment can help us see the law of sacrifice more expansively through the lens of love.

Let's take this idea one step further, into the realm of responsibility and obligation. Like so many things in our modern western culture, the nature of gift giving has changed over time. Today, many would say "a gift" must be freely given, with "no strings attached," but gift giving is a central aspect of human behavior and instinct, it transcends time and place, and it is intrinsically meant to be binding.[2]

Anthropologist Marcel Mauss, an early pioneer in gift theory, recognized that gifts are much more than independent material objects; they also hold symbolic meaning and instill obligations because gift giving encourages reciprocity and cultivates social bonds. It engages the honor and duty of both the giver and the receiver. According to Mauss, "[It] makes the strings between giver and receiver longer and stronger."[3] The obligations a heartfelt gift fosters do not make it *transactional,* they make it *transformational.* Consider how this applies to our covenant relationships with the Lord and with each other. Gifts of the heart are not meant to be paid back, they're meant to be paid *forward;* that God-given feeling of love-fueled duty creates the momentum that lifts our relationships heavenward.

Even a very small child seems to sense this. They have an innate desire to give their parents gifts. In their pure innocence, they give what *they* value most—special treasures, like a recently found feather or a freshly picked dandelion. And though the parent has little need for discarded feathers or troublesome weeds, the sincerity of the sacrifice renders it precious. Because of the childlike love with which it was offered, the parent draws the child closer and gladly honors their caring gesture. Their childlike sincerity can help us learn to be more patient with our attempts to give heartfelt gifts. I can imagine the Lord feeling the same love for each of our sincere offerings, no matter how meager.

As the child grows, they gradually come to understand both sides of the gift-giving coin: the cost of giving up something they personally value *and* the care that goes into determining what *their parent* personally values. Both angles constitute sacrifice. When working in conjunction, they unite the giver and receiver, weaving their hearts together; that tapestry, woven with threads of gifts and offerings, duty and obligation, genuinely given and generously reciprocated, is covenant relationship, and it is "a demonstration of pure love"[4] and a source of true joy.[5]

The lovely relationships of family life are divinely designed to ripple outward, beyond the home, into every realm. Christlike sacrifice can bless every relationship. In that sense, President M. Russell Ballard wisely concluded, "The degree of our love for the Lord, for the gospel, and for our fellowman can be measured by what we are willing to sacrifice for them."[6] This eternal principle, as constant as the laws of mathematics, has infinite ramifications when we consider what has already been sacrificed *for us.*

Jesus Christ is the Gift—perfect, matchless, excellent, and infinite—and God's giving Him declared *our value* as equivalent to *His love:* perfect, matchless, excellent, and infinite (see John 3:16).[7] In other words, the "degree" of God's love for each of us can be "measured" by what He was willing to sacrifice on our behalf.[8] Christ is truly our *Redeemer:* our worth is equal to the price that He paid for our rescue—*infinite, incalculable,* and *priceless.*[9]

Centuries ago, Ignatius of Loyola pondered this relationship and the honor, duty, and obligation that should accompany such an ultimate gift. He thoughtfully concluded, "All things in this world are gifts of God, presented to us so that we can know God more easily and make a return of love more readily."[10] Much more recently, one of Ignatius' faithful modern followers summarized that sentiment beautifully, stating, "When it comes to Kingdom Economics, the only currency that matters in the end is grace and the only return that matters in the end is love."[11] Grace and love are what Christ has so perfectly modeled for us, and therefore what we are commanded to share with each other. In essence, this is the law of sacrifice—to create a relationship, not to make a payment.

Currently, the *General Handbook* articulates the covenant commandment this way: "Obey the law of sacrifice, which means sacrificing to support the Lord's work and repenting with a broken heart and contrite spirit."[12] His gifts are not given simply for our personal enjoyment, to use however we please, but are intended to be used *for His purposes*—to be "paid forward"—and that involves obedience.

President Russell M. Nelson suggested that the laws of

obedience and sacrifice are "indelibly intertwined."[13] Anciently, prior to Jesus Christ's atoning sacrifice on the cross, the children of Israel lived the law of Moses. Its accompanying sacrificial system was very precisely prescribed, so obedience was clearly paramount.

Christ's death and resurrection marked the significant and symbolic shift from animal sacrifice to the bread and water of the sacrament. Though the emblems and ordinances associated with the covenant have changed, the covenant principles remain the same: we still must be obedient in offering our sacrifice. Whether we place a precious animal or our broken heart on the altar, we are being invited "to learn something about ourselves," as President Ballard explained, and that is "what we are willing to offer to the Lord through our obedience."[14] Our gift, freely given, reveals the depth of our love for Him.

In a sense, sacrifice is like amplified obedience. As previously discussed, obedience can feel like stepping onto a bridge into the unknown, unsure why we are being asked to do so but doing it anyway. Sacrifice takes that faith to the next level because "sacrifice" implies an understood cost, even when we don't fully understand the reason for the request; we can still choose to make our small offering. As we do so, we are changed. "We become disciples!" declared President Nelson. "We become more sacred and holy—like our Lord!"[15]

When Eve and Adam were instructed to offer "the firstlings of their flocks" and the first fruits of their harvests, even before they understood why they were doing so, they must have believed it was God's will. They knew God wanted them to do it, and they trusted God. Still, they surely felt the cost acutely—their life literally depended on that food, yet they offered it up anyway (see Moses 5:5–8).[16] Their obedience and sacrifice highlighted their commitment, gratitude, and trust. In our day, we support His work, in part, through our tithes and offerings, which similarly allow us to tangibly acknowledge our faith. We pay tithing because we believe God wants us to, even if we don't completely understand why. In humbly reciprocating God's gifts to us, however disproportionately, our covenant relationship is strengthened, and He sanctifies us.

This is the power of sacrifice memorably described in *Lectures on Faith:* "A religion that does not require the sacrifice of all things never has power sufficient to produce the faith necessary unto life and salvation."[17] Sacrifice is formative; an act of sacrifice shapes our hearts and develops our capacity to hold more love. It allows us to actively participate in and contribute to our most valuable relationships. And it is "a greater investment than any," President Gordon B. Hinckley declared, because "its dividends are eternal and everlasting."[18]

One less discussed aspect of sacrifice is *repentance,* and it, too, is powerful. Though it may feel difficult, and frequently humbling, an apology represents further investment in a relationship. It demonstrates faithful anticipation for forgiveness and reconciliation, as well as one's willingness and desire to change in a positive way.[19] King Lamoni's father exemplified this kind of faith beautifully when he offered his timeless expression of the power of repentance to build divine relationships, declaring to the Lord, "I will give away all my sins to know thee" (Alma 22:15–18). Such an action is "a self-willed change," Elder D. Todd Christofferson taught, one that "respects and sustains our moral agency."[20] It's a way of taking responsibility and going to work, "so that there is something for God to help us with."[21] As one writer observed, "[When] we pay attention to what has gone wrong, we are rewarded with insights of how to do it right."[22] Our commitment to work on our relationship with the Lord opens the door for Him to step in and help us grow closer to Him. Life in a fallen world requires divine assistance; repentance, forgiveness, and grace are crucial components of every heavenly relationship. Our humble, contrite sacrifices reflect Christ's infinite atoning sacrifice for each of us.

This is God's divine design. Jesus Himself directed that each sacrifice we offer reveal some aspect of our wounded and broken heart (see 3 Nephi 9:20).[23] He asks us to vulnerably open our hearts to Him because He was sent to heal and bind up the brokenhearted (see Luke 4:18; Isaiah 61:1). Christ is the Master Healer. "Regardless of the causes of our worst hurts and heartaches," Elder Terrence C. Smith testified, "the ultimate source of relief is the same: Jesus Christ. He alone holds the full power and healing balm to correct every mistake, right every wrong, adjust every imperfection, mend every wound, and deliver every delayed blessing."[24] He is equipped to heal us because of His infinite and perfect love, demonstrated through His ultimate atoning sacrifice.

We are asked to "observe [our] covenants by sacrifice" because that is how He observed His (Doctrine and Covenants 97:8–9). We can offer our whole heart to Him because He has already offered His to us. Accepting the duty and obligations that accompany His matchless gift can strengthen every other relationship, as well; it's an investment of infinite worth and love.

CHAPTER 7

The Way of Christ's Gospel

Christ's gospel is the good news of love. Sister Chieko Okazaki summarized the magnitude of that simple truth conclusively when she wrote, "We live in a world that is held together by love—organized by love, maintained by love, and nurtured by love. Ultimately it will be redeemed by love and even now it is in the process of being redeemed by the love and kindness that we offer each other."[1] Love's glue is God's grace. This grand plan depends on our reliance on Him and on each other.

We are designed for loving companionship with God and one another. The Gospel of Matthew records this dynamic in Jesus's own words: "Thou shalt love the Lord thy God with all thy heart, and with all thy soul, and with all thy mind. This is the first and great commandment. And the second is like unto it, thou shalt love thy neighbour as thyself" (Matthew 22:37–39). Love *is* His law; as President Thomas S. Monson put it, love is "the very essence of [His] gospel."[2]

The phrase "the gospel of Jesus Christ" is synonymous with the phrase "the doctrine of Christ," a connection that sometimes eludes us.[3] We tend to hear "love" in the word "gospel" but "law" in the term "doctrine." Perhaps that is, in part, because we have boiled down the doctrine of Christ, checklist style, to faith, repentance, baptism, receiving the gift of the Holy Ghost, and enduring to the end. In ticking them off on the five fingers of our hand, it's easy to lose sight of the process involved in not only *doing* those things but in *living* that way.

Elder Dale G. Renlund suggested that the key to comprehending the relationship between following the doctrine of Christ and living His gospel is tied to an accurate understanding of "enduring to the end." He explained, "We endure to the end by repeatedly and iteratively 'relying wholly upon' the doctrine and 'merits' of Christ (2 Nephi 31:19)."[4] He then offered some helpful definitions. "'Repeatedly' means that we cycle through the elements in the doctrine of Christ throughout our lives. 'Iteratively' means that we change and improve with each cycle."[5] When done in tandem, they allow us to climb with Christ. He explained God's grace-fueled, transcending power this way: "Even though we cycle repeatedly, we are not spinning in circles. . . . If that were the case, the experience would be dizzying and unproductive. Instead, as we cycle through the elements of the doctrine of Christ, we arrive at a higher plane each time."[6]

Living and loving His gospel means we practice the plan. Our covenant relationships flourish when we choose to *commit, invest*, and *practice*. That three-step dance, done in partnership with the Lord, fosters a graceful, upward spiral that naturally elevates every relationship.

As with each of the five eternal principles we commit to honor and cherish as we exchange covenant promises in the temple, love is both a God-given command—"thou shalt"—*and* a Godlike attribute—love. We might occasionally feel some tension in the relationship between the two. Popular culture typically tells us that we start by having an attribute, and then we act accordingly. But social scientists have found that the formative process more commonly works in the other direction: we start with an action, which then shapes an attribute. What we practice shapes what we love.[7] Prophets affirm this; with every commandment comes the assumption that, with God's help, we can choose how we act (see 1 Nephi 3:7). In other words, by divine design, it's through *doing* that we *become.*

I appreciate how the Living Bible paraphrases 1 John 4:7 because it gently draws this out. "Dear friends, let us practice loving each other, for love comes from God and those who are loving and kind show that they are the children of God, and that they are getting to know him better."[8] *Love takes practice.* And practice is equal parts imitation and participation. When it comes to eternal progression, President Marion G. Romney explained that "it is only through our learning how to take care of each other that we develop within us the Christlike love and disposition necessary to qualify us to return to His presence."[9] Actions often precede attributes; as we follow Christ's example, we become like Him.

In his 2010 conference address, "You Are My Hands," President Dieter F. Uchtdorf described a powerful image of Christ's atoning love, saying, "When I think of the Savior, I often picture Him with hands outstretched, reaching out to comfort, heal, bless, and love." President Uchtdorf then witnessed, "That is what He did during His mortal life; it is what He would be doing if He were living among us today; and it is what we should be doing as His disciples."[10] For me, President Uchtdorf's inspiring testimony evokes the beautiful image of Bertel Thorvaldsen's *Christus*—that glorious marble depiction of the Resurrected Christ with His arms reaching out in love. And though members of The Church of Jesus Christ of Latter-day Saints don't generally focus on the symbol of the cross, the *Christus* subtly reflects what our Christian siblings frequently refer to as "the cruciform shape" of God's love.

The simple diagram of a cross is an enlightening, multilayered symbol of divine love. At the most basic level, the shape illustrates the vertical, heavenward relationship of the first great commandment—to love God—and the horizontal, communal nature of the second—to love our neighbor. Taking it one metaphorical step further, we can highlight some basic engineering elements: first, the vertical beam's primacy. It not only resembles a numeral one, it's also the singular support for the horizontal beam. Without the vertical solidly in place, the horizontal would fall. And second, the integrity of the structure depends on the perpendicular placement of the vertical—literally, its "rightness"—in solid ground. Anything more or less than a ninety-degree angle will compromise its stability. Being square with the Lord aligns our efforts with His, and the result is protection and power. The symbol of the cross reminds us on many levels, in the words of the Apostle John, "We love because He first loved us."[11] Christ leads, and we follow. That crucial pattern involves both imitation and participation—it shapes us as we practice.

Experiential learning is at the heart of mortality. This life is designed to provide the space and time to practice, as well as the three key elements with which to do so: exemplary models to imitate, physical bodies through which to participate, and various objects on which to hone the desired skills. For example, an aspiring pianist seeking to create music like the masters uses his or her hands and a piano. Likewise, a young scientist striving to understand chemicals needs a well-stocked lab in which to experiment. If we are all aspiring to love and serve like the Master, we physically need to practice loving and serving *each other*, and the communal nature of families, neighborhoods, congregations, and communities offers us an optimal celestializing classroom.

We sometimes, however, focus so intently on exaltation's end goal that we inadvertently overlook the way of life that will take us there. Heaven actually begins here, as we work to acquire the skill set that will equip us to eventually live comfortably there.[12] "Service is not something we endure on this earth so we can earn the right to live in the celestial kingdom," Elder Marion G. Romney wisely observed. Rather, "Service is the very fiber of which an exalted life in the celestial kingdom is made."[13] Life is, quite literally, a group service project; it's the learning laboratory of love in which we are being gradually exalted. Just as Jesus "continued from grace to grace," so do we (Doctrine and Covenants 93:13).

Elder Uchtdorf described the transformative power of the practice of service. He taught, "As we extend our hands and hearts toward others in Christlike love, something wonderful happens to us. Our own spirits become healed, more refined, and stronger."[14] That process, persistently practiced between patient people, gradually lifts the whole group, making them "happier, more peaceful, and more receptive to the whisperings of the Holy Spirit."[15] When we commit to love one another and demonstrate our commitment by investing in our relationships—shown by apologizing frequently and forgiving freely as we gradually figure things out—something magical happens! We could call it *celestialization*, a sense of God-supported, synchronized soaring captured by the inspiring Quaker proverb: "Thee lift me, and I'll lift thee, and we'll ascend together."[16]

Our flight is fueled by *reciprocity*, "a mutually beneficial exchange of support that makes each person feel cared for and loved."[17] God loves us and we love Him; then we reach out and love each other.

It's helpful to recognize the vital distinction between reciprocal and transactional: it's the difference between a covenant relationship and a consumer contract. As Rabbi Ari Berman wisely observed, "One of the primary challenges in living in a consumer culture is confusing the two modalities."[18] Participation in a contract implies a balanced interaction, but partners in a covenant strive to give their all to a cooperative one. Likewise, a contract is carefully crafted to allow either party to walk away from troubles, while a covenant is generously designed to help both work through them. Appreciating these distinctions can make the difference between a merely civil relationship and a divine one.

Such gracious interdependence is naturally characterized by sharing, caring, and empathizing. These are the same fruits of covenant relationship Alma described as he stood on the banks of the Waters of Mormon: a willingness and desire to "bear one another's burdens, . . . mourn with those that mourn . . . and comfort those that stand in need of comfort" (Mosiah 18:8–9).[19] That's what it looks like to imitate our perfect Model; we witness Him in our every loving interaction, no matter how imperfect our practice.

CHAPTER 8

The Way of Chastity

Our most divine attribute and our most exalted power. That's how President Dallin H. Oaks has described the magnitude of our God-given ability to create mortal life.[1] Consider this: none of us, as hard as we might try, could ever create a single blade of grass, but we have the capacity, when properly partnered, to create a child. That supreme gift and awesome responsibility—the power of procreation—is governed and guided by the law of chastity, "a single, undeviating standard of sexual morality."[2] Its definition clearly outlines its intended use: "Intimate [sexual] relations are proper only between a man and a woman in the marriage relationship prescribed in God's plan."[3] We might summarize chastity's beautiful blessing and grand command in three simple words: *life is sacred.*[4]

Jesus Christ constantly exhibited this dignified reverence for life. He wept when life was lost and rejoiced when it was restored (see John 11:1–46).[5] His atoning love and sacrifice is the ultimate evidence of life's sanctity; He died "that we might live, and live everlastingly."[6] His mission and ministry is abundant life (see John 10:10). He is Life, and life is sacred (see John 11:25).[7] The dignity of every human soul is at the heart of the law of chastity.

Creating human life is soul work—the bringing together of

spirit and body in the image of God. It is divine partnership with Deity that entails the "greatest privileges and the most weighty responsibilities."[8] Not only are two mere mortals cocreating offspring, but they are simultaneously cocreating an eternal relationship with each other. Elder Richard G. Scott delineated this dual purpose of marital intimacy: "to provide the physical bodies for the spirits Father in Heaven wants to experience mortality" and "to bind husband and wife together in loyalty, fidelity, consideration of each other, and common purpose."[9] That exalting work is far from easy; it's complicated! In fact, Bishop Gérald Caussé proposed that "few earthly experiences require more effort than this: to keep natural physical impulses in harmony with the profound aspirations of the soul."[10] But since our procreative capacity "to kindle other lives" is "the very key" to God's great plan of happiness,[11] we strive to master the paradoxical balance between power and restraint. Living and loving the way of chastity is challenging, but with the Lord's grace and support, it is possible.

Earth's mightiest forces often reflect the cosmic tension between power and restraint. Wind, water, and fire can each create great good or bring about devastating destruction, depending on how their strength is harnessed and controlled. Wind can power a turbine or rip the roof off a house; water can gently carve a beautiful canyon or suddenly wash away a town. Fire carefully tended can warm us or cook a meal, but unleashed can ravenously consume everything in its path.

Likewise, human sexuality, maturely managed, can be some of life's most dynamic, creative energy. Understanding this God-given gift helps us understand the power of chastity, which is essential to the process of ultimately becoming like our heavenly parents.[12] "Our natural affections are planted in us by the Spirit of God, for a wise purpose," wrote Parley P. Pratt in the early days of the

Restoration. "They are the very mainsprings of life and happiness—they are the cement of all virtuous and heavenly society—they are the essence of charity, or love."[13] But as is too often evident, left unchecked, those natural feelings can wreak havoc.

As President Boyd K. Packer explained, "Our happiness in mortal life, our joy and exaltation are dependent upon how we respond to these persistent, compelling physical desires."[14] Such self-control is a vital skill but, when it comes to desire, "self-control" might be a misnomer; living a chaste life "requires more strength than we can muster on our own," wrote Brad Wilcox.[15] Far from being something we can manage alone, it requires God's fortifying grace. Brother Wilcox explained, "By setting bounds, God is not *controlling* us but teaching and empowering us to control ourselves."[16] Agency is always respected, but our patient practice, done in partnership with the Lord, gradually transforms us. We can lean on the Lord in choosing to live this godly lifestyle; He will help us develop a trusting heart and a willingness to sacrifice the easier, more popular path (Proverbs 3:5). As we do so, our faithful habits will eventually lead to our eternal perfection within a heavenly society that we helped to create.

One who lives a chaste life is frequently characterized as "pure" and "clean."[17] Those familiar descriptors might lead us to wonder what soiling impurities we are so actively trying to avoid or rid ourselves of in morality's challenging pursuit. Since antiquity, the Christian devout have warned against the earth's tendency toward corruptibility, recognizing that, like moral gravity, the stuff of this world literally seeks to pull us downward.[18] Transcending the constant tug is hard work that requires our body and spirit to coordinate and cooperate, or, in other words, to respect each other.

Identifying a helpful watchguard against debilitating decay, early Christians named seven vices to guard against—pride, gluttony, lust, greed, envy, anger, and sloth—as well as their seven virtuous counterparts—humility, temperance, chastity, generosity, love, meekness, and diligence.[19] The discipline required to harness and control our natural sexual desires keeps us personally pure and morally clean because it protects us not just from lust but actually fortifies us against all seven of these vicious foes. Gluttony, greed, envy, and anger are frequent companions to unchaste and immoral behavior, as are pridefulness and slothfulness. These baser characteristics are pervasive and persuasive because they are, in a sense, part and parcel of life in a fallen world. There's simply no avoiding getting dirty; dirt is the default. We all fall from time to time. We counteract and overcome them by intentionally developing their seven corresponding virtues—chastity, as well as the six that accompany it. These are *Christlike disciplines* that depend on His help to develop. Thanks to God's gift of grace, when committed to, invested in, and practiced patiently over time, they effectively shape us into His faithful disciples.

This mortal battle "to take control of the physical elements of our lives," according to Bishop Caussé, is "one of the essential objectives of our earthly existence" because it allows our bodies and spirits to "work in harmony to serve higher and eternal purposes."[20] But its benefits are not merely deferred; they lead to true happiness in *this* life, as well, because they foster loving relationships built securely on trust.

Purity matters because we aim for charity, "the pure love of Christ" (Moroni 7:47), even and especially in our most intimate relationships. Dr. Jenet Erickson, family life specialist at Brigham Young University, called that kind of pure love for others "the path of intimacy." In explaining how we are designed for these deepest, loving relationships, she taught, "The Lord's covenant relationship with us is the truest intimacy. It is the experience of perfect love with a Being who we know sees all that we are responsible for—in all our weakness and our sins—and reflects it back to us in the light of His purity, which expands our agency and leads us to a better way through His redeeming love."[21] The path of intimacy is best walked with the Lord as our closest companion.

Nowhere does our individual agency require more careful care and accountability than when it merges with another person's in the most personal of ways, as is the case with sexual intimacy. Because life is sacred, anything that *objectifies, degrades,* or *dehumanizes* ourselves or another does harm. No child of God is a mere object; each is the beloved subject of His most intent concern. Treating either yourself or another as a collection of parts rather than an integrated whole, an object to be used rather than a human to be honored, is at the root of so many of society's worst ailments. As media literacy scholar Dr. Lexie Kite has found through extensive research, "Objectification pushes away love."[22] It diminishes, demeans, and damages relationships on every level.

To overcome these tempting tendencies, we can develop the Christlike attribute of meekness, the ideal antidote to the improper use of power. Imagine a lever balancing the two extremes of coercive control on one end and utter chaos on the end—the point of perfect balance is meekness. Meekness is constructively controlled power, a sure marker for honor and integrity. As peacebuilding professors Patrick Mason and David Pulsipher have observed, "God's honor," securely rooted in His perfect love, righteousness, compassion, and faithfulness, is "the source of God's power and influence in the universe."[23] Just as God demonstrates in honoring our agency, "any durable power or influence over independent moral beings requires their consent and participation."[24]

Every relationship grounded in meekness, honor, and integrity can grow and flourish, powerfully blessing those within its reach.

Meekness is perfectly exemplified by our Savior and King. The way that the Prince of Peace exerts His power is the perfect model for how we should exert ours. Throughout His mortal ministry, and particularly during the events that culminated in His crucifixion, He repeatedly demonstrated meekness by refusing to exert His infinite power for His own personal benefit.[25] One moving example of this was when He was surreptitiously approached by the woman with an issue of blood. Perhaps ostracized by society, she has been identified throughout history only for her disease, but Christ knew her as one of His own. She may have felt deficient—physically, financially, and socially—but her weakness gave her the will to try, and Christ's grace was sufficient to meet her need. Following her courageous act of reaching out to touch His hem, Jesus publicly declared her abundant faith, praising her belief while deflecting attention away from His miraculous power. In doing so, He "reinforced the divine truth surrounding the dignity of all God's children," explained gospel scholar Camille Fronk Olson, "including this seriously marginalized woman," and demonstrated to all who would see the power of the Lord's compassionate, healing touch.[26]

When one is meek, they work to respect and honor others rather than elevate themselves. Elder Bednar's description of meekness captures its majestic essence: "Meekness is strong, not weak; active, not passive; courageous, not timid; restrained, not excessive; modest, not self-aggrandizing; and gracious, not brash."[27] Meekness empowers intimacy while combating domination because it doesn't take advantage of another person's weakness (Ether 12:26). Meekness allows space for creativity, agency, and options for others. It is a generative force for good that is fundamental to building healthy, loving relationships because its unique elements instill trust.

But meekness often feels like an advanced attribute. It must be diligently sought after. It's a spiritual gift that we can prayerfully seek "to benefit and serve the children of God."[28] When it comes to sacred personal relationships—ours or others'—we shun any degree of force, recklessness, or violence, and we actively pursue self-restraint and humble meekness.

The improper use of power can feel easier than the hard work of love. But don't be fooled! That hard work is holy. It "makes possible a richer, a deeper, and a more enduring love of God and of His children," taught Elder Bednar, because "love increases through righteous restraint and decreases through impulsive indulgence."[29] We may struggle to control ourselves completely, but "upon acknowledging our dedication and perseverance," assured Elder Ulisses Soares, "the Lord will give us that which we are not able to attain [on our own] due to our imperfections and human weaknesses."[30] Christ's "grace is sufficient" for every one of us (Ether 12:27). He is our greatest Advocate in this most important, trust-building work.

Our most cherished relationships are built on trust. And chief among those relationships is marriage, which is why scripture so frequently uses the metaphorical language of weddings, like "bride" and "bridegroom," in describing our intended relationship with the Lord.[31] Christ desires to share this kind of complete devotion with each of us. The ancient Hebrew scribes illustrated this degree of devotion, often referred to in scripture as "lovingkindness," with the word *hesed* because its rich meaning "encompasses kindness, mercy, covenant love, and more."[32] *Hesed* is the ultimate term for loyal love.

As President Holland explained, God intended marriage to

exhibit this extent of loyalty and devotion, to be "the *complete* merger of a man and a woman—their hearts, hopes, lives, love, family, future, everything."[33] Like Adam and Eve, "living symbols for all married couples," husband and wife are invited, blessed, and commanded "to be 'one flesh' in their life together."[34] Mutual chastity is essential for the full fusion of two souls; we could not be asked to give our entire self to another without the assurance of our love being fully received and fully reciprocated—total union demands that degree of commitment. *Total* intimacy produces and provides abundance. God intends a "fullness of joy" (Doctrine and Covenants 93:33–34).

Life is sacred; the power to create life is our most divine attribute and our most exalted power.[35] The way of chastity provides safe passage through the natural and challenging storms of life. Practiced with meekness, a chaste lifestyle protects us and those we love, as well as those we *ever hope* to love. The trust it develops blesses every relationship. Living and loving like Jesus Christ depends on devoted obedience as a way of life, as well as a willingness to sacrifice immediate personal pleasure for deferred shared joy. We can faithfully do both when we keep our focus on love of God and love of others.

CHAPTER 9

The Way of Consecration

Fundamentally, consecration entails taking something mundane and making it holy, something Jesus did frequently.[1] He turned water into wine (see John 2:1–11), multiplied a boy's meager lunch to feed a multitude (see John 6:5–14), and used dirt to heal (John 9:1–7). Elder D. Todd Christofferson described consecration as "set[ting] apart" something as sacred.[2] In a more personal sense, Elder David A. Bednar characterized it as "a commitment [to be] developed for holy purposes," or making ourselves "fit for use and fully available" to assist in God's work.[3] As the *General Handbook* explains, the law of consecration calls for the dedication of our "time, talents, and everything with which the Lord has blessed [us]" to the sacred purpose of "building up Jesus Christ's Church on the earth."[4] As the culminating covenant of the five, it's the highest ideal with the furthest reach.

Through consecration we partner and participate in God's great work. Christ longs to collaborate with us in making the wounded whole.[5] Living a consecrated lifestyle allows us to participate in God's boundless power and infinite capacity to bless and heal His entire eternal family through devoted love.

One intriguing example of such dedicated discipleship is found in the story of Elijah passing his prophetic mantle to Elisha in 2 Kings. You might recall that the ancient prophet Elijah has a particular affinity for familial love and loyalty. In 1836, in fulfillment of prophecy, Elijah stood before Joseph Smith and Oliver Cowdery and restored the sealing authority in this dispensation, "to turn the hearts of the fathers to the children, and the children to the fathers" (Doctrine and Covenants 110:15).[6]

Many centuries earlier, as he concluded his mortal ministry, Elijah had asked his disciple Elisha what he would like from him before he was taken up to heaven (2 Kings 2:9–15). Elisha's singular request is instructive: he asked for *a double portion* of the Spirit. That's kinship language—the language of family—and it is Elijah's specialty. "A double portion" points to the birthright, which was usually given to the oldest son to help him care for the entire family. The birthright designation was significant because it provided for the ongoing care of the family. If a family had four children, the father would typically divide his inheritance into *five* parts—one for each, plus a *second* for the child who held the birthright. At the father's death, or in his absence, the birthright child would assume the father's authority but also his many responsibilities and obligations, including providing for and watching over the rest of their kin. So, yes, much was given but even more was required in return (Luke 12:48).[7] Elisha's request for "a double portion" reflects his sincere desire to devote *everything* to his relationship with God and others. It signifies his complete love and loyalty to his Father and his Father's family.

In fact, the idea of "much," though a small and perhaps overused word, has some grand gospel implications when it comes to embracing the way of consecration. The modern English word "much" is our translation of the ancient Hebrew term *me'od.* It is an adverbial intensifier that heightens and magnifies the idea that follows, which is often effectively translated as "very," "greatly," or "exceedingly," though in one key passage it might actually be best expressed as *muchness.*[8]

The beloved Jewish prayer called the Shema, recorded in Deuteronomy 6:5, memorably highlights the idea of *muchness*. In this verse, the King James Version translates *me'od* as "might," like this: "And thou shalt love the Lord thy God with all thine heart, and with all thy soul, and with all thy *might.*"[9] Whether we think of this first great commandment as requiring "might," "mind," or "strength," the combination of those ideas is trying to get at the idea of our *entirety*—literally our whole *selves*, from every angle—our *muchness.* In other words, as one scholar explained, "The point is that everything in a person's life—every moment, every opportunity, every ability, and capacity—offers a chance to love and honor the One who made you."[10] This is the big idea of living and loving Christ's way of consecration; it's the love of a loyal child.

So with "muchness" in mind, let's return to the definition of *consecration*. Dedicating something to a high and holy purpose implies an alternative: one might choose *not* to do something for such noble reasons, perhaps opting for lowly self-gratification instead. In other words, when it comes to what motivates us, there's always an underlying choice involved. That's why gospel scholar Barbara Morgan Gardner aptly summed up consecration as "agency at its finest."[11]

But recognizing the crucial role of our agency in consecration draws out an important distinction worth noting. We do not make ourselves holy or sacred; rather, we willingly offer ourselves—"our time, talents, and everything with which the Lord has blessed" us[12] (in short, our *muchness*)—to God and allow *God* to sanctify our offering.[13] As Elder Bednar reminds us, "Our limited mortal capacity is completely insufficient to ever realize our eternal possibilities."[14] Hence, "we need and depend upon the grace, strength, inspiration, and means that only the Lord can provide."[15] But He provides His grace, strength, inspiration, and means so freely! As Elder Bednar emphasized, "*Every* facet of God's work is designed to develop and bless His sons and daughters."[16] As we assist Him in His work,[17] by offering *all* that we are and *all* that we have, in a wide variety of ways, "every act of selfless service that we render helps us become more acquainted with the Master whom we represent, and every act draws us closer to Him."[18]

But *all* starts with *any.* Something is always better than nothing, so even when we feel our simple offering is sorely inadequate, when given sincerely, it is enough. That's how consecration works. In retelling the well-known story of the widow's mite, Elder Dieter F. Uchtdorf reiterated that "our offering may be large or it may be small," what matters is that it is "our *heartfelt all.*"[19] Just as Christ made an example of the widow's faith, He pleads with us to bring Him what we can, no matter how meager, so He can make it mighty. As Sister Michelle Craig helpfully reminded us, "Jesus's miracles often begin with a recognition of want, need, failure, or inadequacy."[20] The divine economy graciously allows for such grossly imbalanced returns—though we offer little, He bestows much; He transforms our ordinary into His extraordinary.

God invites us to give up the world's law of scarcity and adopt His law of abundance. Like the prodigal's father, He begs us, His children, to believe Him when He insists, "All that I have is thine" (Luke 15:31). He asks that we reflect His great abundance and respond in kind with heartfelt faith. He promises that when we willingly share everything He has blessed us with, in the spirit of *muchness*, there will always be "enough and to spare" (Doctrine and Covenants 104:17).[21]

So how might we expand our vision to see how truly all-encompassing consecration's *muchness* is meant to be? Adopting two relatively straightforward perspective shifts can benefit us in profound ways.

First, we can replace a premature mentality of ownership with a humble stance of stewardship, remembering "where all came from and whose all is."[22] Consider, when we pray, do we thank Heavenly Father for *our* blessings or for *His*? How we phrase that common sentiment might depend on our primary language, but it may also reflect our default disposition.[23] We might remind ourselves more frequently to ask, like the Psalmist, "What shall I render unto the Lord for all his benefits toward me?" (Psalms 116:12).

The basis for this humble stance is quite simple: everything we have comes from God.[24] Acknowledging this eternal truth is beneficial because, as educator Richard Eyre has helpfully observed, while an ownership paradigm reminds one constantly of self, a stewardship paradigm redirects one's focus constantly toward God.[25] Ultimately, He would like to give us, as His heirs, everything He has, but for now, our stewardship is a precursor to and preparation for that eventual possibility; the final outcome depends on our faith-filled participation.[26]

In the meantime, He can *always* make more out of our lives than we can. As President Ezra Taft Benson broadly illustrated, God can "deepen [our] joys, expand [our] vision, quicken [our] minds, strengthen [our] muscles, lift [our] spirits, multiply [our] blessings, increase [our] opportunities, comfort [our] souls, raise up friends, and pour out peace."[27] As the Savior taught, "Whoever will lose his life for my sake shall find it" (Matthew 16:25). The scriptures demonstrate that repeatedly.[28] Truly, we are doubly blessed!

The second suggestion for living and loving a more consecrated way of life is to broaden your understanding of generosity, stewardship's close cousin. Generosity is about so much more than giving a few dollars away; it's an *attitude* that can be applied to every gift, talent, strength, and resource.

We can strive to be more generous with our time, our affection, our compliments, and even our apologies; for me, that means consecration often looks like patience. We can work at being more generous with our attention by listening with both ears and our whole heart. Of course, we can generously share our comforts—little luxuries that make life more pleasant—but we can also share our *dis*comforts, vulnerably opening up about our challenges and struggles. On the surface, that might not seem particularly generous, but to someone who is silently suffering, assuming they are "the only one," that might be the greatest gift you could give.

Generosity shares its prefix *gen-* with words like *generation, genus*, and *genesis*, indicating the idea of creation, or being of one kind.[29] Applying that insight, theologian Henri Nouwen noted that "generosity is a giving that comes from the knowledge of that intimate bond" of kinship. Christlike generosity has the power to build the kingdom of God, creating the family it believes in.[30]

A culture of consecration is an indispensable feature of every thriving community. A citizenry comprised of generous stewards lies at the heart of every model society, whether we name that lofty pursuit of peace Zion, the Beloved Community, the City of God, or Shalom.[31] Effective community organizers, from modern prophets and saints to medieval preachers and rabbis, strive to reach up to God and bring heaven down to earth. The proponents of each ideal believe that their goal is actually *achievable*, that a society of peace and love *can* be built if enough of its citizens embrace God's two great commandments—loving God and loving neighbor. They are absolutely, gloriously right: *this is Christ's way,* and with His help, it *can* be done. As President Russell M. Nelson has urged us to recognize, "The Savior's message is clear: His *true* disciples build, lift, encourage, persuade, and inspire."[32] Working together, "we can literally change the world—one person and one interaction at a time."[33] Heaven begins here, and we get to build it.

The more interdependent and interconnected community members are, the more organically we can assist each other in our building project. Our progress—yours and mine and everyone else's we interact with—is necessarily interwoven because that's the nature of agency. When one moves, many do. Individual agency rarely means isolated results; it more often means far-reaching repercussions.

In this respect, perhaps the law of consecration is as much about receiving as it is about giving. As a wise friend once mused, when we give our time to our friends, we are blessed to receive theirs in return. When we share our talents with them, we enjoy theirs as well. The way of consecration illustrates that "we do not have to know it all, be it all, have it all, or do it all" to experience the greatness of all God has created, given, and offered.[34]

Certainly, creating heaven on earth is no ordinary calling, but, in the spirit of consecration, President Wilford Woodruff wisely observed, "every act of our lives should be performed with this in view."[35] Ours is meant to be a life of service, of intentionally building the kingdom of God, as demonstrated by Jesus Christ.[36] In the late eighteenth century, John Wesley, one of the founders of the Methodist movement, expressed this same sentiment when he penned these memorable lines:

Do all the good you can,
By all the means you can,
In all the ways you can,
In all the places you can,
At all the times you can,
To all the people you can,
As long as you ever can.[37]

The Lord will help us love like this—with *muchness*—through our covenant relationship with Him, nurtured in His holy house, and with every other relationship beyond its four walls. This is the "great work" we are called to be instrumental in undertaking. And, in doing so, as the Prophet Joseph promised, "He will endow [us] with power, wisdom, might and intelligence, and every qualification necessary."[38] That's the beauty of consecration, the culminating characteristic of the five eternal principles of loving relationships we practice in the temples and with each other: it works both ways.

In an address she titled "God's Covenant of Peace," Sister Patricia T. Holland expressed this power of divine reciprocity beautifully, testifying, "At the same time we covenant with God, *He is covenanting with us*—promising blessings, privileges, and pleasures our eyes have not yet seen and our ears have not yet heard."[39] Gratefully, His gifts are *not* dependent on our perfection; they are a function of input, not outcome, as she goes on to explain. "Though we may see *our* part in the matter of faithfulness going by fits and starts, by bumps and bursts here and there, *God's* part is sure and steady and supreme. We may stumble, but He never does. We may falter, but He never will. We may feel out of control, but He never is."[40] Our covenant relationships "forge a link between our telestial mortal struggles and God's celestial immortal powers."[41] God graciously bridges the gap between what we know and what we do—when we willingly work with Him, He meets us where we are and refines what we want, sanctifying our hearts in the process.[42]

The law of consecration reflects one of the crowning promises of our covenant relationship with God: when we strive to give Him our all, whatever that may look like—including our trusting obedience, humble sacrifice, service to others, and reverence for life—He can take all our experiences and use them for our good (see Romans 8:28–30).[43] When we offer our all to God, He gives us much more in return.

CHAPTER 10

Atoning Love

In *Death Comes to the Archbishop*, novelist Willa Cather tells the story of two dear friends, Catholic priests striving to create a faithful, frontier community in nineteenth-century America. Following a moment of quiet reflection, one confides to the other, "I do not see you as you really are." With love as his lens, he observes, "I see you through my affection for you." As they ponder this reality, they realize that "where there is great love there are always miracles."[1] That's because the power of divine love is able to not only purify our intentions but also refine our perceptions, "so that, for a moment, our eyes can see and our ears can hear what is there around us always."[2] That great constant, always there and always around us, even amid the many vicissitudes of life, is Jesus Christ's atoning love.[3]

President Jeffrey R. Holland offered an encompassing definition of the Atonement of Jesus Christ. "[It is] the central fact, the crucial foundation, the chief doctrine, and the greatest expression of divine love in the eternal plan of salvation."[4] The Lord's expansive love is the basis for our eternal gathering to Him and each other. As the Apostle Paul wrote to the Ephesians, God will "gather together in one all things in Christ, both which are in heaven, and which are on earth; even in him" (Ephesians 1:10). That gathering, as President Russell M. Nelson has repeatedly taught, is the most important work in the world.[5] Christ's mission is the "renewed relationship of all to all."[6] His atoning love—His work of *at-one-ment*—reconciles, unites, restores, and heals. His grace makes us whole. That "first great truth" can become our ultimate comfort and our primary motivation to join Him in His work.[7]

Such enhanced perception changes everything. We see miracles when we trust in His constant love. "When you know and understand how completely you are loved as a child of God," explained President Susan H. Porter, "it changes the way you feel about yourself when you make mistakes [and] when difficult things happen. It changes your view of God's commandments [and] your view of others and of your capacity to make a difference."[8] By placing Him solidly at the center of our lives, "at the core of our thoughts and deeds,"[9] we synchronize ourselves with God's love and "discover the strength to overcome, the courage to persevere, and the peace that surpasses all understanding."[10] With Him as our prime focus, rather than sensing a hundred little things competing for our time, we can concentrate on one—"loving and serving God and His children, in a hundred different ways."[11]

This Christ-centric alignment is an endowment of love we receive as we worship in the house of the Lord, and then we leave with what we learned, clothed in the garment of the holy priesthood, literally wrapped in that love.[12] Though we might like to stay in God's warm, secure, comfortable house, we go to the temple to make covenants, and then we leave to live them.[13] We take His empowering presence with us and go create that love-filled sense of belonging within our own homes and relationships. The sacred privilege to wear the holy garment is a departing gift to help us in our quest and to remind us continually of the Giver.[14] The very constancy of our wearing it symbolizes His ever-present care. The temple garment is a tangible reminder that helps us "feel His limitless love for us and learn to love Him in return."[15]

That additional layer of clothing corresponds to an added layer of meaning as we bear witness to a deepening desire for both His closeness and His influence, and the associated obedience and sacrifice intensify the message. The wordless language of clothing is a highly effective form of communication.[16] After all, "fashion" is both a noun and a verb; it's one of many ways we humans differentiate ourselves from our peers and style our identities. Our wardrobe broadcasts our preferences *and* shapes our personality. The daily decision to underlay each outfit with a layer of His love forms us in His image as we go along our way, living His gospel day by day.

Additionally, the holy garment testifies to the sanctity of the body. Like the coats of skin prepared for Eve and Adam prior to their departure from the Garden of Eden, God's desire to daily dress our physical frame in a protective token of His love reminds us that our soul is so much more than spirit; it is interwoven spirit *and* body. Their interdependence and ultimate reunion are why resurrection and exaltation are the ultimate goal! Our powerful doctrine of the body admonishes us to honor and care for it because it is the vehicle through which we experience life and feel God's love. Wearing the sacred garment—literally *feeling* it against our skin, at any given moment—emphasizes how profoundly God values our body and inspires us to do likewise. It can serve as a transformative tool as we honor our covenant commitments because it tangibly incorporates the eternal principles of obedience, sacrifice, chastity, and consecration, as we live and love the gospel of Jesus Christ.

Our holy hope is for covenant collaboration with Deity, every day and in every way. Our physically enacted, personally signified, embodied commitments, like symbols deeply lived,[17] help us "use our gifts and capabilities with greater intelligence and increased effectiveness in order to bring to pass our Heavenly Father's purposes in our own lives and the lives of those we love."[18] Gratefully, we can return to the temple frequently to reignite that "veritable explosion of spiritual, moral power" that President Holland described that gives us "the ability, the capacity, the will, and the way" to love each other as God loves us.[19] As we choose to take upon ourselves His name and His nature by embracing the eternal principles of loving relationships, we gradually become like Him.[20] Christ's covenant way of living and loving is the pathway to peace. It's a public trail that was made for us to enjoy together, sometimes slowing down to walk alongside a friend, sometimes holding a neighbor's hand as she struggles to climb the next hill, and occasionally pausing to smell some roses or examine a dandelion with a child. These simple and sacred moments of life are the roots and fruits of eternal relationships.

The Lord invites us to delight in His abundant love, personally, individually, and communally. Christ's covenant way of living and loving is happiness. Living and loving His way, with our whole hearts, is how we build heaven on earth.

I delight to do thy will, O my God:
yea, thy law is within my heart.

PSALM 40:8

Acknowledgments

Writing about the transcendent power of divine love and covenant relationships has only been possible because of the many supportive souls who have modeled and extended such transcendent love to me. I am deeply grateful to each of them for their generous friendship and faith, and profoundly thankful for our Savior who makes covenant relationships possible.

I'm thankful for my parents, who instilled in me a love for the temple as far back as I can remember. Every few months, they'd leave for a few days on the temple-trip bus from Belmont to Washington, D.C. Their devotion to the Lord and desire to spend time with Him in His holy house planted a precious seed that they've nourished carefully ever since. Thank you, Mom and Dad, for your joyful and tireless temple service.

My love for temple worship has blossomed and flourished thanks to my dear husband, our four children, their terrific spouses, our five grandsons, and our extended family. The love we share inspires me to keep striving, returning often to the Lord's house to practice and internalize the life-changing eternal principles that continually strengthen our relationships. I adore each of you and look forward to spending the rest of eternity together.

I'm thankful for a sisterhood that brightens my every day.

Women need women, and I'm surrounded by outstanding ones. I cherish our laughter and tears and everything in between. Special thanks to Candace, Allie, Rachel, Cristin, Alison, Mandy, Kristy, and Emily for helping me complete this project during an intense season; I could not have done it without each of you and your gentle support, thoughtful wisdom, and enthusiastic encouragement.

I'm grateful for the team at Deseret Book—especially Lisa Roper, Michelle Torsak, Janiece Johnson, and Kristen Evans. Thank you for helping me share my personal witness of God's love more broadly. And I'm so thankful for Justin Wheatley's artistic talents, which packaged my thoughts so beautifully.

Finally, I express my sincere gratitude to my leaders and friends in the Provo YSA 4th Stake and for the opportunity to teach Temple+ to the dearest students imaginable. The light in your eyes and love for the Lord is contagious. You have blessed me, and I'm confident you will bless the world.

Notes

INTRODUCTION

1. Henri Matisse, "Looking at Life with the Eyes of a Child," in *The UNESCO Courier* 49, no. 5 (1996): 50.
2. Tracy Y. Browning, "Seeing More of Jesus Christ in Our Lives," *Liahona,* November 2022.
3. See J. Ballard Washburn, "The Temple Is a Family Affair," *Ensign,* May 1995.
4. "The Living Christ: The Testimony of the Apostles," Gospel Library; emphasis added.

CHAPTER 1: FEELING AT HOME IN THE HOUSE OF THE LORD

1. Thomas S. Monson, "We Never Walk Alone," *Ensign,* November 2013.
2. The Prophet Joseph Smith shared his personal experiences with this influential character trait, declaring: "Nothing is so much calculated to lead people to forsake sin as to take them by the hand and watch over them with tenderness. When persons manifest the least kindness and love to me, O what pow'r it has over my mind, while the opposite course has a tendency to harrow up all the harsh feelings and depress the human mind." Joseph Smith, Jr., address to the Nauvoo Female Relief Society, 9 June 1842, "Nauvoo Relief Society Minute Book, 62, The Joseph Smith Papers, https://www.josephsmithpapers.org/paper-summary/minutes-and-discourse-9-june-1842/2.
3. M. Russell Ballard, "Let Our Voices Be Heard," *Ensign,* November 2003.

4. Tamara W. Runia, "Seeing God's Family through the Overview Lens," *Liahona,* November 2023.
5. Ellen Davis and Margaret Adams Parker, *Who Are You, My Daughter?* (Louisville: Westminster John Knox Press, 2003), 19. See Brown-Driver-Briggs Hebrew and English Lexicon, 629.
6. Davis and Parker, *Who Are You, My Daughter?*, 19.
7. Dallin H. Oaks, "Kingdoms of Glory," *Liahona,* November 2023.
8. "Abide with Me!" *Hymns of The Church of Jesus Christ of Latter-day Saints*, no. 166.
9. Oxford English Dictionary, "abode."
10. Russell M. Nelson, "Choices for Eternity" (worldwide devotional for young adults with President Nelson, 15 May 2022), https://www.churchofjesuschrist.org/study/broadcasts/worldwide-devotional-for-young-adults/2022/05/12nelson?lang=eng#title1.
11. Nelson, "Choices for Eternity."
12. Nelson, "Choices for Eternity."
13. Jeffrey R. Holland, "The Message, the Meaning, and the Multitude," *Ensign,* November 2019; see also Russell M. Nelson, "The Temple and Your Spiritual Foundation," *Liahona,* November 2021.
14. Holland, "The Message, the Meaning, and the Multitude."
15. Holland, "The Message, the Meaning, and the Multitude." President Holland further expounded on this important principle, stating, "When one goes to the holy temple for the first time, he or she may be somewhat awestruck by that experience. Our job is to ensure that the sacred symbols and revealed rituals, the ceremonial clothing and visual presentations, never distract from but rather point toward the Savior, whom we are there to worship. The temple is His house, and He should be uppermost in our minds and hearts—the majestic doctrine of Christ pervading our very being just as it pervades the temple ordinances—from the time we read the inscription over the front door to the very last moment we spend in the building. Amid all the wonder we encounter, we are to see, above all else, the meaning of Jesus in the temple."

CHAPTER 2: BUILDING ON THE ROCK

1. See also Genesis 49:24; Doctrine and Covenants 50:44.
2. See also 2 Nephi 9:45; Jacob 7:25.
3. See Jeffrey R. Holland, "The Message, the Meaning, and the

Multitude," *Ensign,* November 2019. See also David A. Bednar, "Be Still and Know That I Am God," *Liahona*, May 2024.
4. Russell M. Nelson, "The Temple and Your Spiritual Foundation," *Liahona,* November 2021.
5. D. Todd Christofferson, "Free Forever, to Act for Themselves," *Ensign,* November 2014.
6. Fred P. Edie and Mark A. Lamport, *Nurturing Faith* (Grand Rapids: Eerdmans Publishing Co., 2021), 17.
7. Terry Ball and Nathan Winn, *Making Sense of Isaiah: Insights and Modern Applications* (Salt Lake City: Deseret Book, 2009), 70. Dr. Terry Ball, former dean of Religious Education at BYU, penned the following: "Expressed simply, the covenant promises that if we follow Heavenly Father's plan, we can become like Him. The everlasting covenant includes many principles and ordinances, such as the new and everlasting covenant of marriage and the new and everlasting covenant of baptism. In some periods of history some aspects of the covenant have varied. For example, in Abraham's day the covenant included ordinances of circumcision and blood sacrifice. In our dispensation it includes the ordinance of the sacrament. Despite these slight differences, the promise of the covenant has been consistent in all ages. If we follow God's plan, we can become as He is."
8. Russell M. Nelson, "The Everlasting Covenant," *Liahona,* October 2022.
9. Christofferson, "Free Forever, to Act for Themselves."
10. Russell M. Nelson, "We Are Children of God," *Ensign,* November 1998; see also Doctrine and Covenants 88:15.
11. See Genesis 8:11 and Genesis 9:9–17.
12. See Matthew 3:16; Luke 3:22; and John 1:32.
13. See Doctrine and Covenants 88:125.
14. See Doctrine and Covenants 20:73, "Having been commissioned of Jesus Christ, I baptize you in the name of the Father, and of the Son, and of the Holy Ghost. Amen."
15. Though much used, this phrase was popularized by Dr. Maya Angelou.
16. David A. Bednar, "Ye Must Be Born Again," *Ensign,* May 2007.
17. Bednar, "Ye Must Be Born Again."
18. Bednar, "Ye Must Be Born Again."
19. Bednar, "Ye Must Be Born Again."

20. Patrick Kearon, "God's Intent Is to Bring You Home," *Liahona,* May 2024.
21. See David A. Bednar, "The Hearts of the Children Shall Turn," *Ensign,* November 2011.

CHAPTER 3: BECOMING BILINGUAL

1. Marva A. Bennett, *To Love Is to Act: 'Les Misérables' and Victor Hugo's Vision for Leading Lives of Conscience* (Chicago: Swan Isle Press, 2020). Victor Hugo is the literary mastermind behind the compassionate masterpiece *Les Misérables,* in which he wrote, "To love another person is to see the face of God."
2. President Jeffrey R. Holland has defined moral agency as "the moral and intellectual ability to distinguish right from wrong and the attendant freedom to make choices based on that knowledge." *Christ and the New Covenant: The Messianic Message of the Book of Mormon* (Salt Lake City: Deseret Book, 1997), 200.
3. David O. McKay, in Conference Report, April 1950, 32, https://catalog.churchofjesuschrist.org/assets/d3eefcfa-0a24-41a6-a85b-46cf404e532a/0/33?lang=eng.
4. Joseph Fielding Smith, *Doctrines of Salvation*, vol. 1, 70.
5. Dale G. and Ruth Lybbert Renlund, *The Melchizedek Priesthood: Understanding the Doctrine, Living the Principles* (Salt Lake City: Deseret Book, 2018), 116.
6. George Q. Morris, in Conference Report, April 1958, 41, https://catalog.churchofjesuschrist.org/assets/81c72ca8-1dc2-445d-8fbf-df1543804d81/0/40?lang=eng.
7. C. S. Lewis, *Mere Christianity* (New York: HarperOne, 1952), 48.
8. Theologian-philosopher James K. A. Smith expounds on this idea thoroughly in his excellent book *You Are What You Love: The Spiritual Power of Habit* (Grand Rapids: Brazos Press, 2016).
9. *Oxford English Dictionary*, "liturgy." Though members of the Church don't frequently use this term in speaking about the ordinances and covenants of the temple, in a broader, theological sense, *liturgy* describes any group worship experience that follows a precise and repeated script or patterned experience. Such sacred rites are also broadly referred to as *rituals.*
10. Elder Dale G. Renlund taught, "The covenants God established were not whimsical or capricious but were based on eternal, unchanging law." Dale G. Renlund, "Stronger and Closer Connection

to God through Multiple Covenants" (Brigham Young University—Idaho devotional, 22 October 2023), byui.edu/speeches.

11. Renlund, "Stronger and Closer Connection to God through Multiple Covenants."
12. Russell M. Nelson, "The Love and Laws of God" (Brigham Young University devotional, 17 September 2019), speeches.byu.edu.
13. Boyd K. Packer, "Atonement, Agency, Accountability," *Ensign,* May 1988.
14. Tad R. Callister, *The Infinite Atonement* (Salt Lake City: Deseret Book, 2000), 151–52.
15. See *General Handbook: Serving in the Church of Jesus Christ of Latter-day Saints,* 27.2, Gospel Library, https://www.churchofjesuschrist.org/study/manual/general-handbook/27-temple-ordinances-for-the-living?lang=eng.
16. President Dallin H. Oaks explained, "To help us develop the godly attributes and the change in nature necessary to realize our divine potential, the Lord has revealed doctrine and established commandments based on eternal law. . . . The covenants made and the blessings promised to the faithful in the temples of God are the key." Dallin H. Oaks, "Divine Love in the Father's Plan," *Liahona,* April 2022.
17. Russell M. Nelson, "The Temple and Your Spiritual Foundation," *Liahona,* November 2021.
18. Nelson, "The Temple and Your Spiritual Foundation."
19. Terry Ball and Nathan Winn, *Making Sense of Isaiah: Insights and Modern Applications* (Salt Lake City: Deseret Book, 2009), 70.
20. *Brown-Driver-Briggs Hebrew and English Lexicon,* 1036; see also Jeff Benner, *Ancient Hebrew Language and Alphabet* (College Station: Virtualbookworm.com Publishing Inc, 2004), 16–17. The most ancient meaning of *shamar* is closely tied to a sheepfold, referring to the way a shepherd attentively watches over their flock.
21. Richard G. Scott, "To the Lonely and Misunderstood" (Brigham Young University devotional, 10 August 1982), speeches.byu.edu.
22. Gary Chapman, *The Five Love Languages: The Secret to Love That Lasts* (Chicago: Northfield Publishing, 2015), 142.
23. M. Russell Ballard, "Lovest Thou Me More Than These?" *Liahona,* November 2021.

CHAPTER 4: SHARING THE LOVE AND SHARING THE LOAD

1. Dr. Bill Sears, "11 Ways to Teach Your Child to Share," www.askdrsears.com, https://www.askdrsears.com/topics/parenting/discipline-behavior/morals-manners/11-ways-teach-your-child-share/.
2. Alma describes some of the fruits of the baptismal covenant, illustrating what a covenant community looks like in action. See Mosiah 18:21.
3. Dale G. Renlund, "Stronger and Closer Connection to God through Multiple Covenants" (Brigham Young University—Idaho devotional, 22 October 2023), byui.edu/speeches; emphasis added.
4. Kristen M. Yee, "Our Covenant Relationship with God: A Wellspring of Relief" (Brigham Young University devotional, 24 October 2023), speeches.byu.edu.
5. See Mosiah 18:8–16.
6. *General Handbook: Serving in The Church of Jesus Christ of Latter-day Saints*, 27.2, Gospel Library, https://www.churchofjesuschrist.org/study/manual/general-handbook/27-temple-ordinances-for-the-living?lang=eng.
7. David A. Bednar, "Receive the Holy Ghost," *Ensign*, November 2010.
8. Terryl Givens, "'Lightning Out of Heaven': Joseph Smith and the Forging of Community" (Brigham Young University forum, 29 November 2005), speeches.byu.edu.
9. *General Handbook: Serving in The Church of Jesus Christ of Latter-day Saints,* 27.2.
10. *General Handbook: Serving in The Church of Jesus Christ of Latter-day Saints*, 26.3.3.1.
11. Spencer W. Kimball, "Privileges and Responsibilities of Sisters," *Ensign,* November 1978.
12. Joy D. Jones, "Value beyond Measure," *Ensign,* November 2017, emphasis added.
13. Thomas S. Monson, "We Never Walk Alone," *Ensign,* November 2013, emphasis added.
14. Patrick Kearon, "God's Intent Is to Bring You Home," *Liahona*, May 2024; see 2 Nephi 19:21 (Isaiah 9:21); 20:4 (Isaiah 10:4); 15:25 (Isaiah 5:25); Hebrews 4:14-16; see also Emma Lou Thayne, "Where Can I Turn for Peace?," *Hymns of the Church of Jesus Christ of Latter-day Saints*, no. 129, verse 3.

15. See Clark G. Gilbert, "Becoming More in Christ: The Parable of the Slope," *Ensign,* November 2021. See also Brad R. Wilcox, "Worthiness Is Not Flawlessness," *Ensign,* November 2021. Brother Wilcox defined "worthiness" as "being honest and trying," and then compassionately emphasized that "His grace is not just a prize for the worthy. It is the 'divine assistance' He gives that helps us become worthy. It is not just a reward for the righteous. It is the 'endowment of strength' that helps us become righteous."
16. Cecil O. Samuelson, "Be Ye Therefore Perfect" (Brigham Young University devotional, 6 September 2011), speeches.byu.edu. President Heber J. Grant spoke to this crucial difference, as well, saying, "Nobody lives up to his ideals, but if we are striving, if we are working, if we are trying, to the best of our ability, to improve day by day, then we are in the line of our duty. If we are seeking to remedy our own defects, if we are so living that we can ask God for light, for knowledge, for intelligence, and above all for His spirit, that we may overcome our weaknesses, then, I can tell you, we are in the straight and narrow path that leads to life eternal; then we need have no fear." See Conference Report, April 1909, 111, https://catalog.churchofjesuschrist.org/assets/a2fd2a2d-3296-4cac-9e1c-948ac080fd0c/0/112.
17. Russell M. Nelson, "Perfection Pending," *Ensign,* November 1995.
18. Nelson, "Perfection Pending."
19. Nelson, "Perfection Pending"; emphasis added.
20. Renlund, "Stronger and Closer Connection to God through Multiple Covenants." Notably, Elder Renlund was extremely precise in articulating the distinction between the "specific commitments" of baptism ("to serve God, to keep His commandments, and to be willing to take upon us the name of Jesus Christ") and the "fruits" of the baptismal covenant, or "what a converted soul would naturally do" ("bear one another's burdens, mourn with those that mourn, and comfort those that are in need of comfort").
21. Charles L. Tyer, "Yoke," *The Anchor Yale Bible Dictionary*, ed. David Noel Freedman (New Haven: Yale University Press), 1992.
22. Charles L. Tyer, "Yoke," *The Anchor Yale Bible Dictionary.*
23. Charles L. Tyer, "Yoke," *The Anchor Yale Bible Dictionary.*
24. David A. Bednar, "Bear Up Their Burdens with Ease," *Ensign,* May 2014; see also Matthew 11:28–30.
25. See 1 Nephi 11–14. Similarly, the Lord repeatedly taught the early

Saints, through His prophet Joseph Smith, that they would be "endowed with power from on high." See also Doctrine and Covenants 38:38; 43:16; 95:8; 105:11.

26. Russell M. Nelson, "Spiritual Treasures," *Ensign,* November 2019.
27. Russell M. Nelson, "Choices for Eternity" (worldwide devotional for young adults with President Nelson, 15 May 2022), https://www.churchofjesuschrist.org/study/broadcasts/worldwide-devotional-for-young-adults/2022/05/12nelson?lang=eng. See also Russell M. Nelson, "Drawing the Power of Jesus Christ into Our Lives," *Ensign,* May 2016.

INTERLUDE

1. *Oxford English Dictionary*, "temple," "template," "contemplate," "pattern," "patron." See also *The American Heritage Dictionary of Indo-European Roots,* ed. Calvert Watkins (Boston: Houghton Mifflin Harcourt, 2011), 93.
2. Jamie Ann Steck, "Cutting a Covenant: Making Covenants and Oaths in the Old Testament and the Book of Mormon," *Studia Antiqua* 4, no. 1 (2005), https://scholarshipsarchive.byu.edu/studiaantiqua/vol4/iss1/2.
3. *Oxford English Dictionary*, "pattern."
4. Robert D. Hales, "Coming to Ourselves: The Sacrament, the Temple, and Sacrifice in Service," *Ensign,* May 2012.
5. Hales, "Coming to Ourselves: The Sacrament, the Temple, and Sacrifice in Service."
6. Dale G. Renlund, "Stronger and Closer Connection to God through Multiple Covenants" (Brigham Young University devotional, 5 March 2024), speeches.byu.edu.
7. Renlund, "Stronger and Closer Connection to God through Multiple Covenants."
8. Renlund, "Stronger and Closer Connection to God through Multiple Covenants." See also Dale G. Renlund, "Accessing God's Power through Covenants," *Liahona,* May 2023.
9. See Matthew 1:5, where Rahab (*Rachab*) is included as one of the significant women in Matthew's genealogical record of Jesus Christ. Note that Rahab and her family were eventually incorporated or adopted into the family of Israel.
10. The Hebrew word used here is *'ot*, interestingly defined as a sign or signal, such as a flag, beacon, monument, evidence, mark, or

miracle. And the "true" that describes Rahab's requested "token" is the Hebrew *emet*, defined as truth, faithfulness, reliability, or sureness, reflecting certain stability, loyalty, or commitment. *Brown-Driver-Briggs Hebrew and English Lexicon,* 16, 54.

11. *Brown-Driver-Briggs Hebrew and English Lexicon,* 876. *The Hebrew and Aramaic Lexicon of the Old Testament,* Ludwig Koehler and Walter Baumgartner (Leiden: Koninklijke Brill NV, 2001), 1781–83.
12. Additionally, in pondering Rahab's red thread, we might consider how the scarlet color symbolizes the Savior's atoning love and sacrifice on each of our behalf.
13. Of course, the nature of multiple strands can work both ways, as Satan's "flaxen cord" that Nephi describes in 2 Nephi 26:22 signifies; we must choose wisely *which* strings we would like attached.
14. Elder Dale G. Renlund has addressed this aspect of iterative covenants repeatedly, including in his excellent BYU—Idaho devotional, "Stronger and Closer Connection to God through Multiple Covenants," 22 October 2023. In that message, he counseled, "Let the multiple covenants draw you closer to Heavenly Father and Jesus Christ and strengthen your covenantal bonds with Them." Also worth noting, Elder Renlund emphasized that "being bound to the Savior does not mean we are enslaved, coerced, shackled, or under compulsion." Rather, "agency remains operative."
15. Elder Renlund defined the covenant path as "the series of covenants through which we come unto Christ and connect to Him and our Heavenly Father." Renlund, "Stronger and Closer Connection to God through Multiple Covenants."
16. Renlund, "Stronger and Closer Connection to God through Multiple Covenants."
17. Kristen M. Yee, "Our Covenant Relationship with God: A Wellspring of Relief" (Brigham Young University devotional, 24 October 2023), speeches.byu.edu.
18. Samuel M. Brown, *First Principles and Ordinances* (Provo: Neal A. Maxwell Institute for Religious Scholarship, 2014), 153.

CHAPTER 5: THE WAY OF OBEDIENCE

1. See Peter H. Miller, "Architecture of Ascension," 25 May 2022, https://www.traditionalbuilding.com/opinions/architecture-of-ascension.

2. Russell M. Nelson quoting David O. McKay in "Overcome the World and Find Rest," *Liahona,* November 2022, footnote 14.
3. Dale G. Renlund, "Stronger and Closer Connection to God through Multiple Covenants" (Brigham Young University—Idaho devotional, 22 October 2023), byui.edu/speeches.
4. The Manti Temple was dedicated in 1888 by the prophet Wilford Woodruff. *The Manti Temple Centennial* (1988) describes these two staircases as "the work of superb nineteenth-century craftsmen," being two of "only three stairways in the United States constructed with no central support and of [such] a large size." Each has "151 steps supporting [each] other" and is "wide enough for four men to walk abreast."
5. Dallin H. Oaks, "The Plan and the Proclamation," *Ensign,* November 2017.
6. See Clark G. Gilbert, "Becoming More in Christ: The Parable of the Slope," *Ensign,* November 2021.
7. Richard G. Scott, "The Fruits of Obedience" (Brigham Young University devotional, 3 June 1990), speeches.byu.edu.
8. D. Todd Christofferson, "The Power of Covenants," *Ensign,* May 2009, footnote 2.
9. Christofferson, "Power of Covenants," emphasis added.
10. See *General Handbook: Serving in The Church of Jesus Christ of Latter-day Saints,* 27.2, Gospel Library.
11. Jeffrey R. Holland, "The First Great Commandment," *Ensign,* November 2012.
12. W. H. Murray, *The Scottish Himalayan Expedition* (London: J. M. Dent & Sons, 1951), 6–7.
13. Pete Davis, *Dedicated* (New York: Avid Reader Press, 2021), 48.
14. D. Todd Christofferson, "Moral Agency" (Brigham Young University devotional, 31 January 2006), speeches.byu.edu.
15. Terry Ball and Nathan Winn, *Making Sense of Isaiah: Insights and Modern Applications* (Salt Lake City: Deseret Book, 2009), 70.
16. Pete Davis, *Dedicated.*
17. Willa Cather, *Willa Cather on Writing: Critical Studies on Writing as an Art* (Lincoln, NE: of Nebraska Press, 1988), 123.
18. D. Todd Christofferson, "The Power of Covenants," *Ensign,* May 2009.
19. Ezra Taft Benson, "The Great Commandment—Love the Lord," *Ensign,* May 1988.

20. L. Tom Perry, "Obedience through Our Faithfulness," *Ensign,* May 2014.
21. Andy Stanley and Lane Jones, *Communicating for a Change* (New York City: Multnommah, 2006), 98.
22. See also Jacob 4:15–17. See also 2 Samuel 23:3; Isaiah 17:10; 1 Corinthians 10:4.
23. Thomas Aquinas, *Commentary on the Gospel of John, Chapters 13–21,* translated by Fabian Larcher and James A. Weisheipl (Washington, DC: Catholic University of America Press, 2010), 109.

CHAPTER 6: THE WAY OF SACRIFICE

1. David Cheal, "'Showing Them You Love Them': Gift Giving and the Dialectic of Intimacy," *The Sociological Review* 35, 1: 150, https://onlinelibrary.wiley.com/doi/abs/10.1111/j.1467-954X.1987.tb00007.x.
2. Iver Mysterud, et al, "An Evolutionary Interpretation of Gift-Giving Behavior in Modern Norwegian Society," *Evolutionary Psychology* 4, 1 (2006), https://journals.sagepub.com/doi/10.1177/147470490600400132.
3. Mysterud, "An Evolutionary Interpretation of Gift-Giving Behavior in Modern Norwegian Society." This idea is fundamental to Mauss's classic work, *The Gift*, written in 1925; see Marcell Mauss, *The Gift: The Form and Reason for Exchange in Archaic Societies*, translated by W. D. Halls (New York: W. W. Norton, 1990).
4. M. Russell Ballard, "The Blessings of Sacrifice," *Ensign,* May 1992.
5. See Carol B. Thomas, "Sacrifice: An Eternal Investment," *Ensign,* May 2001.
6. Ballard, "The Blessings of Sacrifice."
7. See also 1 John 4:10; Romans 6:23; 2 Corinthians 9:15; Ether 12:11; "The Living Christ: The Testimony of the Apostles," Gospel Library.
8. Ballard, "The Blessings of Sacrifice."
9. I am indebted to Area Seventy Elder Jed Jake Hancock who made this point powerfully in an address given to the Provo YSA 4th Stake on 10 March 2024.
10. Ignatius Loyola, "The First Principle and Foundation," in David Fleming, *Spiritual Exercises of St. Ignatius: A Literal Translation and a Contemporary Reading,* 2nd ed. (Brighton, MA: Institute of Jesuit Sources, 1978).
11. Ryan Tafilowski, "Kingdom 'Economics': What is Stewardship?"

www.denverinstitute.org, https://www.denverinstitute.org/kingdom-economics-what-is-stewardship/.

12. *General Handbook: Serving in The Church of Jesus Christ of Latter-day Saints*, 27.2, Gospel Library, https://www.churchofjesuschrist.org/study/manual/general-handbook/27-temple-ordinances-for-the-living?lang=eng.
13. Russell M. Nelson, "Lessons from Eve," *Ensign,* November 1987.
14. Ballard, "The Law of Sacrifice."
15. Nelson, "Lessons from Eve."
16. See also Exodus 23:16, 19.
17. *Lectures on Faith* (Salt Lake City: Deseret Book, 1985), 69.
18. Gordon B. Hinckley, *Teachings of Gordon B. Hinckley* (Salt Lake City: Deseret Book, 1997), 567–68.
19. See Dale G. Renlund, "Lifelong Conversion" (Brigham Young University devotional, 14 September 2021), speeches.byu.edu; and John H. Groberg, "The Beauty and Importance of the Sacrament," *Ensign,* May 1989.
20. D. Todd Christofferson, "Free Forever, to Act for Themselves," *Ensign,* November 2014.
21. Christofferson, "Free Forever, to Act for Themselves."
22. Cecilia Gonzalez-Andrieu, *Bridge to Wonder* (Waco: Baylor University Press, 2012), 129.
23. See also Doctrine and Covenants 59:8.
24. Terrence C. Smith, "An Anatomy of Troubles" (Association of Mormon Counselors and Psychotherapists Convention, October 2008), https://salifeline.org/wp-content/uploads/2016/11/An-Anatomy-of-Troubles-by-Terrence-Smith-for-SA-Lifeline-website.pdf. At the time of this outstanding address, Dr. Smith, a physician, was serving as an Area Seventy in Raymond, Albert, Canada.

CHAPTER 7: THE WAY OF CHRIST'S GOSPEL

1. Chieko N. Okazaki, *Being Enough* (Salt Lake City: Bookcraft, 2002), 10.
2. Thomas S. Monson, "Love—the Essence of the Gospel," *Ensign,* May 2014.
3. Dale G. Renlund, "The Powerful, Virtuous Cycle of the Doctrine of Christ," *Liahona,* May 2024, footnote 7.
4. Dale G. Renlund, "Lifelong Conversion" (Brigham Young University devotional, 14 September 2021), speeches.byu.edu.

5. Renlund, "Lifelong Conversion."
6. Renlund, "Lifelong Conversion."
7. James K. A. Smith, *You Are What You Love: The Spiritual Power of Habit* (Grand Rapids: Brazos Press, 2016).
8. See *The Living Bible,* BibleGateway.com, https://www.biblegateway.com/passage/?search=1%20John%204%3A17&version=TLB
9. Marion G. Romney, "Living Welfare Principles," *Ensign,* November 1981.
10. Dieter F. Uchtdorf, "You Are My Hands," *Ensign,* May 2010.
11. 1 John 4:19, NRSV. It is worth noting that the King James Version of the New Testament is one of the few that renders that verse, "We love *him* because he first loved us" (emphasis added), based on some ambiguity in the ancient Greek, as well as subtle differences in manuscript tradition. See personal correspondence with Dr. Amy Krall, ThD, in the possession of the author.
12. See Dallin H. Oaks, "Kingdoms of Glory," *Liahona,* May 2023.
13. Marion G. Romney, "The Celestial Nature of Self-Reliance," *Ensign,* November 1982.
14. Dieter F. Uchtdorf, "You Are My Hands," *Ensign*, May 2010.
15. Uchtdorf, "You Are My Hands."
16. This frequently quoted proverb is commonly attributed to Quaker poet John Greenleaf Whittier (1807–1892).
17. Kendra Cherry, MSEd, "What is Reciprocity?" March 7, 2023. www.verywellmind.com, accessed March 11, 2024, https://www.verywellmind.com/what-is-the-rule-of-reciprocity-2795891.
18. Ari Berman, "Covenant vs Consumer Education" (Brigham Young University forum, 31 January 2023). See also Bruce C. Hafen, "Covenant Marriage," *Ensign*, November 1996.
19. See also Dale G. Renlund, "Stronger and Closer Connection to God through Multiple Covenants" (Brigham Young University—Idaho devotional, 22 October 2023), byui.edu/speeches.

CHAPTER 8: THE WAY OF CHASTITY

1. Dallin H. Oaks, "The Great Plan of Happiness," *Ensign,* November 1993.
2. David A. Bednar, "We Believe in Being Chaste," *Ensign,* May 2013.
3. Bednar, "We Believe in Being Chaste"; see also "The Family: A Proclamation to the World," Gospel Library; and *General Handbook:*

Serving in The Church of Jesus Christ of Latter-day Saints, 27.2, Gospel Library.

4. See James E. Faust, "The Sanctity of Life," *Ensign,* May 1975. See also Joseph F. Smith, *Juvenile Instructor* 53:182–83, April 1918, https://catalog.churchofjesuschrist.org/assets/c82abcb2-a554-4bf7-a254-64caed50b763/0/0.
5. See also Luke 8:49–56.
6. Thomas S. Monson, "Gifts," *Ensign*, May 1993.
7. See John 14:6.
8. Faust, "The Sanctity of Life."
9. Richard G. Scott, "Making the Right Choices," *Ensign,* November 1994.
10. Gérald Caussé, "Harmony of Body and Spirit: A Key to Happiness" (Brigham Young University devotional, 13 October 2020), speeches.byu.edu.
11. Boyd K. Packer, "Cleansing the Inner Vessel," *Ensign,* November 2010.
12. See Dale G. and Ruth L. Renlund, "The Divine Purposes of Sexual Intimacy," *Liahona,* August 2020.
13. Parley P. Pratt, *Writings of Parley Parker Pratt,* 52–53, as cited in *Eternal Marriage Student Manual,* https://www.churchofjesuschrist.org/study/manual/eternal-marriage-student-manual/intimacy-in-marriage?lang=eng#p9.
14. Boyd K. Packer, "The Plan of Happiness," *Ensign,* May 2015.
15. Brad Wilcox, *Changed Through His Grace* (Salt Lake City: Deseret Book, 2017), 59.
16. Wilcox, *Changed Through His Grace*, 59.
17. See Jeffrey R. Holland, "Personal Purity," *Ensign,* November 1998; and Russell M. Nelson, "Personal Preparation for Temple Blessings," *Ensign,* May 2001.
18. Tsh Oxenreider, *Bitter and Sweet* (Eugene: Harvest House Publishers, 2022), 21–24; see also 2 Peter 1:4.
19. Oxenreider, *Bitter and Sweet*, 21–24; see also 2 Peter 1:4.
20. Caussé, "Harmony of Body and Spirit: A Key to Happiness."
21. Jenet Jacob Erickson, "Designed for Covenant Relationship" (Brigham Young University devotional, 8 November 2022), speeches.byu.edu.
22. Lexie Kite, "Objectification and Loving Relationships Are Not

Compatible," morethanabody.org, https://www.morethanabody.org/objectification-loving-relationships-incompatible/.
23. Patrick Q. Mason and J. David Pulsipher, *Proclaim Peace: The Restoration's Answer to an Age of Conflict* (Salt Lake City: Neal A. Maxwell Institute for Religious Scholarship and Deseret Book Company, 2021), 7.
24. Mason and Pulsipher, *Proclaim Peace: The Restoration's Answer to an Age of Conflict,* 7.
25. For example, see Matthew 4:1–11; 9:20–22; 26:51–55; Mark 5:25–34; Luke 8:43–48; 22:47–51; John 8:3–11; 13:1–17; 18:10–15; 20:11–18.
26. Camille Fronk Olson, *Women of the New Testament* (Salt Lake City: Deseret Book, 2014), 195–197.
27. David A. Bednar, "Meek and Lowly of Heart," *Ensign,* May 2018.
28. Bednar, "Meek and Lowly of Heart."
29. David A. Bednar, "We Believe in Being Chaste," *Ensign*, April 2013; see also Doctrine and Covenants 121:36–37.
30. Ulisses Soares, "Be Meek and Lowly of Heart," *Ensign,* November 2013.
31. See, for example, Isaiah 61:10; 62:5; Jeremiah 33:11; Matthew 9:15; 22:1–14; 25:1; John 3:29; Revelation 21:2, 9; Doctrine and Covenants 33:17; 65:3; 88:92; 109:74.
32. Russell M. Nelson, "The Power of Spiritual Momentum," *Liahona,* May 2022. President Russell M. Nelson has spoken of *hesed* frequently in teaching of covenant love; see Russell M. Nelson, "The Everlasting Covenant," *Liahona,* October 2022. See also Psalm 36:7; Isaiah 63:7; Jeremiah 31:3; Hosea 2:19. The story of the prophet Hosea shares some of sacred writ's most expansive thoughts related to the power of *hesed.*
33. Jeffrey R. Holland, "Personal Purity," *Ensign,* November 1998.
34. Jeffrey R. Holland, "Of Souls, Symbols, and Sacraments" (Brigham Young University devotional, 12 January 1988), speeches.byu.edu. See also Genesis 2:23–24.
35. Dallin H. Oaks, "The Great Plan of Happiness," *Ensign,* November 1993.

CHAPTER 9: THE WAY OF CONSECRATION

1. *Oxford English Dictionary*, "consecration."

2. D. Todd Christofferson, "Reflections on a Consecrated Life," *Ensign*, November 2010.
3. David A. Bednar, speaking at the Alamodome in San Antonio, Texas, 11 November 2018, as shared by @davidabednar, 19 November 2018.
4. *General Handbook: Serving in The Church of Jesus Christ of Latter-day Saints*, 27.2, Gospel Library, https://www.churchofjesuschrist.org/study/manual/general-handbook/27-temple-ordinances-for-the-living?lang=eng.
5. Dale G. Renlund, "Family History and Temple Work: Sealing and Healing," *Ensign*, May 2018.
6. David A. Bednar, "The Hearts of the Children Shall Turn," *Ensign*, November 2011; see also Malachi 4:6; Luke 1:17; 3 Nephi 25:6.
7. See also Doctrine and Covenants 82:3.
8. *Brown-Driver-Briggs Hebrew and English Lexicon*, 547; for example, Genesis 1:31; Genesis 7:18; Genesis 17:2. See also *The Hebrew and Aramaic Lexicon of the Old Testament*, 1581–86.
9. Emphasis added. Interestingly, when Jesus reiterates this commandment in Mark 12:30, the Anglicized Greek of the New Testament has Him express this as a combination of "mind" and "strength."
10. Jon Collins and Tim Mackie, "What It Means to Love God with 'All Your Strength,'" BibleProject.com, https://www.youtube.com/watch?v=9aaVy1AmFX4.
11. Barbara Morgan Gardner, *Follow Him* podcast, episode 17, part 2, originally aired 17 April 2021, https://followhim.co/episodes-1-20/.
12. *General Handbook: Serving in The Church of Jesus Christ of Latter-day Saints*, 27.2, Gospel Library, https://www.churchofjesuschrist.org/study/manual/general-handbook/27-temple-ordinances-for-the-living?lang=eng.
13. See Doctrine and Covenants 11:20 and its corollary, Moses 1:39.
14. David A. Bednar, "'Consider the Wondrous Works of God' (Job 37:14" (Brigham Young University devotional, 23 January 2024), speeches.byu.edu.
15. Bednar, "'Consider the Wondrous Works of God' (Job 37:14)."
16. Bednar, "'Consider the Wondrous Works of God' (Job 37:14)," emphasis added.
17. See Doctrine and Covenants 6:9.
18. Bednar, "'Consider the Wondrous Works of God' (Job 37:14)."
19. Dieter F. Uchtdorf, "Our Heartfelt All," *Liahona*, May 2022.

20. Michelle Craig, "Divine Discontent," *Ensign*, November 2018.
21. Like all invitations to live a higher law, its application varies depending on context. Anciently, the Israelites followed the laws of gleaning, leaving a portion of their crops unharvested for those in need (see Ruth 2). In the early days of the Restoration, the Saints lived the United Order (see Doctrine and Covenants 104). As Elder D. Todd Christofferson noted, "The Lord's law of consecration . . . has an economic role but, more than that, is an application of celestial law to life here and now." D. Todd Christofferson, "Reflections on a Consecrated Life," *Ensign*, November 2010. For a much deeper dive into these historical applications, see Steven C. Harper, *Let's Talk About the Law of Consecration* (Salt Lake City: Deseret Book, 2022).
22. Richard Eyre, *Stewardship of the Heart* (Ink, Inc.: 1990), iii. Elder Christofferson called our life on earth "a stewardship of time and choices granted by our Creator." See Christofferson, "Reflections on a Consecrated Life."
23. For example, in German, the common idiom is "thank Thee for your many blessings."
24. See Psalm 24:1; Alma 5:40. Elder Orson Pratt taught, "In the consecrating that which we have been in the habit of calling our own, we are only returning to the Lord His own property." Orson Pratt, "Consecration," in *Journal of Discourses*, vol. 2 (1855): 99, https://contentdm.lib.byu.edu/digital/collection/JournalOfDiscourses3/id/7952.
25. Eyre, *Stewardship of the Heart*, 104.
26. See Romans 8:17; 1 Corinthians 6:19–20; Galatians 3:29; 4:7; Titus 3:7; James 2:5; Mosiah 115:11; Abraham 1:2. See also Dallin H. Oaks, "Kingdoms of Glory," *Liahona*, November 2023.
27. Ezra Taft Benson, "Jesus Christ—Gifts and Expectations" (Brigham Young University devotional, 10 December 1974), speeches.byu.edu.
28. For example, the stories of Joseph of Egypt (Genesis 39–46), the prophet Enoch (Moses 6–8), and Alma the Younger (Mosiah 27–28), among countless others.
29. *Oxford English Dictionary*, "generosity," "generation," "genus," "genesis."
30. Henri Nouwen, *The Return of the Prodigal Son: A Story of Homecoming* (New York: Doubleday, 1992), 131–32.
31. Dr. Martin Luther King, Jr., wrote and spoke extensively about

the idea of creating a beloved community, which has been described as "a community in which everyone is cared for, absent of poverty, hunger, and hate" (Grace Tatter, "Achieving King's Beloved Community," Harvard Graduate School of Education, 18 January 2019, https://www.gse.harvard.edu/ideas/news/19/01/achieving-kings-beloved-community). See Dr. King's Palm Sunday Sermon on Mohandas K. Gandhi, delivered at Dexter Avenue Baptist Church, Montgomery, Alabama, 22 March 1959, https://kinginstitute.stanford.edu/king-papers/documents/palm-sunday-sermon-mohandas-k-gandhi-delivered-dexter-avenue-baptist-church. See also Andrew Teal, "Building a Beloved Community" (Brigham Young University forum, 26 October 2021), speeches.byu.edu. In the early fifth century, Augustine wrote of a city that prioritizes love of God and is predestined for salvation, calling it the City of God; see Augustine of Hippo, *De Civitate Dei Contra Paganos* [Concerning the city of God against the pagans] (Western Roman Empire: AD 426). *Shalom* is the Jewish term for God's intent for creation; see Amy L. Sherman, *Agents of Flourishing: Pursuing Shalom in Every Corner of Society* (Downers Grove, IL: InterVarsity Press, 2022).

32. Russell M. Nelson, "Peacemakers Needed," *Liahona*, May 2023.
33. Nelson, "Peacemakers Needed."
34. Taylor Ricks, personal correspondence with the author.
35. Wilford Woodruff, "Epistle to the Saints, 6 April 1888," 2, The Wilford Woodruff Papers, https://wilfordwoodruffpapers.org/documents/642d2d05-38cf-46f6-99bc-e693cfa22a1a/page/5b80f0d5-1d07-4512-a332-36f5739ce5b8. See also Doctrine and Covenants 24:7; 30:11.
36. D. Todd Christofferson, "Reflections on a Consecrated Life," *Ensign*, November 2010.
37. John Wesley, George Eayrs, and Augustine Birrell, *Letters of John Wesley* (London: Hodder and Stoughton, 1915), 423.
38. Joseph Smith, Jr., History, 1838–1856, volume C-1 [2 November 1838–31 July 1842], https://www.josephsmithpapers.org/paper-summary/history-1838-1856-volume-c-1-2-november-1838-31-july-1842/230.
39. Patricia T. Holland, "God's Covenant of Peace" (Brigham Young University Women's Conference address, May 1999), https://womens

conference.byu.edu/sites/womensconference.ce.byu.edu/files/holland_patricia.pdf.
40. P. Holland, "God's Covenant of Peace."
41. P. Holland, "God's Covenant of Peace."
42. See Helaman 3:35.
43. See also 2 Nephi 2:2; 32:9; Doctrine and Covenants 90:24; 122:7.

CHAPTER 10: ATONING LOVE

1. Willa Cather, *Death Comes to the Archbishop* (New York: Union Square & Co., 1927), 36.
2. Cather, *Death Comes to the Archbishop.*
3. Elder Jose L. Alonso taught, "He is the living water, fulfilling the deepest needs of our souls with His constant love and kindness," Jose L. Alonso, "Jesus Christ at the Center of Our Lives," *Liahona,* May 2024; see also Christofferson, "The Love of God," *Liahona,* November 2021; Bonnie D. Parkin, "Eternally Encircled in His Love," *Ensign,* May 2006; and Gordon B. Hinckley, "Let Love Be the Lodestar of Your Life," *Ensign,* May 1989.
4. Jeffrey R. Holland, *Christ and the New Covenant: The Messianic Message of the Book of Mormon* (Salt Lake City: Deseret Book, 1997), 197.
5. Russell M. Nelson, "Hope of Israel" (worldwide youth devotional, 3 June 2018); Russell M. Nelson, "Let God Prevail," *Ensign,* November 2020; Russell M. Nelson, "Overcome the World and Find Rest," *Liahona,* November 2022.
6. Cecilia Gonzalez-Andrieu, *Bridge to Wonder* (Waco: Baylor University Press, 2012), 17.
7. Jeffrey R. Holland, "The Greatest Possession," *Liahona,* November 2021; see also 1 John 4:19.
8. Susan H. Porter, "God's Love: The Most Joyous to the Soul," *Liahona,* November 2021.
9. Alonso, "Jesus Christ at the Center of Our Lives."
10. Alonso, "Jesus Christ at the Center of Our Lives."
11. Dieter F. Uchtdorf, "Our Heartfelt All," *Liahona,* May 2022.
12. See Alonso, "Jesus Christ at the Center of Our Lives"; see also 2 Nephi 1:15.
13. See J. Ballard Washburn, "The Temple Is a Family Affair," *Ensign,* May 1995.
14. Dallin H. Oaks, "Covenants and Responsibilities," *Liahona,* May

2024; see also J. Anette Dennis, "Put Ye On the Lord Jesus Christ," *Liahona,* May 2024.

15. Tracy Y. Browning, "Remember, Remember," (First Presidency's Christmas devotional, 3 December 2023).
16. See Lauren F. Winner, *Wearing God: Clothing, Laughter, Fire, and Other Overlooked Ways of Meeting God* (New York: Harper One, 2015), 31–61.
17. See Thomas M. Finn, *Early Christian Baptism and the Catechumenate: West and East Syria* (Collegeville, MN: Liturgical, 1992), 5.
18. David B. Haight, "Come to the House of the Lord," *Ensign,* May 1992.
19. Jeffrey R. Holland, "The Greatest Possession," *Liahona*, November 2021.
20. See Jennifer C. Lane, *Let's Talk about Temples and Ritual* (Salt Lake City: Deseret Book, 2023).

About the Author

MELINDA W. BROWN is an author and educator. She has a master's degree in Christian Practice from Duke Divinity School with an emphasis in Christian Education. She is the author of *Eve and Adam: Discovering the Beautiful Balance* (Deseret Book, 2020), and a frequent contributor to the Magnify podcast and *LDS Living*. She enjoys every minute spent teaching young adults about learning to love the temple. She has a passion for deep discussions with faithful followers of Christ who are seeking joy, even amid life's thorny patches. Mindy and her husband Doug have four children and five grandchildren. Her perfect day would include playing with all of them, exploring along the beach, digging into a stack of books, and sharing delicious treats.